LIFE ABUNDANTLY

Life Abundantly: *How Loss Taught Me How to Live*

Copyright © 2022 Arlene Zandbelt

All rights reserved.

No part of this publication may be reproduced in a retrieval system, or transmitted in any form or by any means—electronic, mechanical, photocopying, recording, or otherwise—without the prior written permission of the publisher.

This manuscript has undergone viable editorial work and proofreading, yet human limitations may have resulted in minor grammatical or syntax-related errors remaining in the finished book. The understanding of the reader is requested in these cases. While precaution has been taken in the preparation of this book, the publisher and author assume no responsibility for errors or omissions, or for damages resulting from the use of the information contained herein.

Scriptures taken from the Holy Bible, New International Version®, NIV®. Copyright © 1973, 1978, 1984, 2011 by Biblica, Inc.™ Used by permission of Zondervan. All rights reserved worldwide. www.zondervan.com The "NIV" and "New International Version" are trademarks registered in the United States Patent and Trademark Office by Biblica, Inc.™ Scripture taken from the New King James Version®. Copyright © 1982 by Thomas Nelson. Used by permission. All rights reserved. The Holy Bible, English Standard Version® (ESV®) Copyright © 2001 by Crossway, a publishing ministry of Good News Publishers. All rights reserved. ESV Text Edition: 2016. Scripture quotations marked (NLT) are taken from the Holy Bible, New Living Translation, copyright ©1996, 2004, 2015 by Tyndale House Foundation. Used by permission of Tyndale House Publishers, Carol Stream, Illinois 60188. All rights reserved.

This book is set in the typeface *Athelas* designed by Veronika Burian and Jose Scaglione.

Paperback ISBN: 9798846250765

A Publication of *Tall Pine Books*
119 E Center Street, Suite B4A | Warsaw, Indiana 46580
www.tallpinebooks.com

| 1 22 22 20 16 02 |

Published in the United States of America

LIFE ABUNDANTLY

How Loss Taught Me How to Live

Arlene Zandbelt

"Heart-felt, Inspiring & Compelling. This book, this message, is a powerful display of Gods heart cry to his people to LIVE and to live abundantly. Don't hesitate, don't let comfort, worry, or fear lead, let God. As the author says "Choose today to turn down the volume on the voice of fear and tune into the whisper of faith. It is not too late." Don't wait. GO NOW.

This is a book people will read not just once, it will be highlighted, circled, and tagged as it becomes a growth manual to many. Thank-you Arlene for stepping out and sharing your gift.

—Christine Bobye,
Business Owner, friend, and mentee for 12 year

"I have known Arlene for 10 years and as she is in life, so she is in this book. Real. Real about the cost of trauma, the confusion of grief and the comfort of faith. Her words of encouragement are a genuine invitation to dream and to do so in the face of tragedy and fear. It's a reminder that the difficulties of life can either cripple us or be the catalyst to thriving. I'm grateful for this invitation to believe in greater things to come, I know you will be too.

—Heather Holt

"I have known Arlene for 10 years and I can testify about many of the accounts narrated in this book. I have seen her develop spiritually and fearlessly pursue this incredible journey beyond the bounds of religious comfort and passive Christianity. This book is a breath of fresh air, a call to action, and a beacon of Hope announcing to the reader 'no you are not crazy, there is more to your Sunday church Christian life! It is a real and raw exposition of the many fears we face when trying to step out of our comfort zone, but it also offers practical and simple ways to get started on this great adventure.

—Angelo Nwigwe

This book was written in memory of my beautiful, creative, passionate big sister, Kathy. Thank you for loving me unconditionally without judgement or expectations. I miss you so much.

The thief comes only to steal and kill and destroy. I came that they may have LIFE and have it abundantly.

JOHN 10:10 ESV

CONTENTS

Foreword ix
Introduction xi

1. The Day that Changed Everything 1
2. Becoming a Sister 5
3. The Great Loss 15
4. It's Okay to Inconvenience People...People that You Love ... 21
5. You ARE Loved! Now believe it! 25
6. Live by Faith not Fear 35
7. Make God Your Partner 45
8. Write It Down 57
9. Don't Wait to Do What You Love 73
10. Let God Heal Your Heart 87
11. God Intended it For Good 95
12. But I am not Strong Enough 103
13. As He Speaks 117
14. There will always be reasons not to 123
15. Now Go Ahead, Live Life Abundantly 129

Inner Healing Resources 137

FOREWORD

"Let my heart be broken by the things that break the heart of God," Bob Pierce.

THERE ARE TIMES in our lives when the Lord moves us in a different direction than the one, we believed was our path. In these times, I believe the Lord places people in our lives that shift our perspectives. They see in us what we cannot even begin to see for ourselves. Over the last 14 years of friendship with Arlene, she has been like a sister to me and more than a blessing in my life as she saw the light in me when all I could see was darkness. Watching her walk with the Lord, through all of life's unexpected challenges, has taught me resiliency, determination, and compassion. She stands for truth; she fights for her friends, family, and the people of God's Kingdom. Through her story in this book, you will learn how to partner with the mighty power of Jesus to walk in your healing and freedom, while being encouraged that you are not alone on this journey.

I remember the day Arlene called me to tell me about Kathy. I recall the moments of prayer that followed. The gatherings, the laying on of hands contending for Kathy's healing, and the tears of loss when the battle was lost in this world and Kathy went home to be with Jesus. I never quite know how to support a loved one during a time of loss. It's heart breaking to be in the pain with them. But we, as her friends and family, gathered around her, spoke life into her, held her when she needed us most, and covered her in prayer and love as Arlene walked out the pain of loss and disappointment.

Arlene didn't allow her loss to pull her farther away from the Lord and her purposes. It was almost like it added fuel to her already burning passion to save and heal Jesus' lost sheep. She did not allow the enemy to steal her dreams and her destiny. Arlene's message of hope in the following pages will encourage you to walk the journey to freedom. A journey that places God at the center of your life and challenges you to face the fears that are holding you back. We only have one life to live on this earth. Listen to where God is calling you, step out of your "comfort zone" as she says, and go live an abundant life so you can change the world around you!

ALICIA CREVIER

INTRODUCTION

OUR PRESENT CHRISTIAN Culture has defined what a "good Christian life" should look like for too long. It has confined Christians in a box for long enough. We have become imprisoned by what religion has decided is a "good Christian life" and **it is time to set the captives FREE!**

Set free from the expectations others have for us. Set free from the limitations we've placed on ourselves. Set free from accepting an average life. John 10:10 does not say " I have come that they may have life and have it averagely." He came for you to have life abundantly. If we are truly walking with Jesus and living the life that he has planned for us, our lives should be anything but average. Consider the disciples who walked with Jesus, their days were filled with adventure. They never knew what would happen next. Would the lame get up and walk? Would bread multiply to feed thousands? Would the blind man see again? And after Jesus returned to heaven and the Holy Spirit came, what was that like? 3000 people came to believe in Jesus in ONE DAY! Now that is exciting! In the last 2000 years Christianity went from this great adventure to going to church on Sunday. What happened? Now there is nothing wrong with regular church attendance but there is more available to us if we choose it. If we, like the disciples, choose to follow his lead. The disciples chose to put Him first. Above their professions, above their families, above their comfort. Because they were available, God was able to use their gifts and talents to do great things in the world.

The picture of the "Good Christian" going to church on Sunday, raising a nice family, going to a safe job on Monday, paying the mortgage and putting money in the offering plate each week needs to be radically shaken up. Walking with Jesus looked nothing like that 2000 years ago. Christianity wasn't a Sunday thing; it was an everyday thing. If Jesus went, they followed. Why are we satisfied with only scratching the surface of what God has for us?

Why miss out on the adventure God has for us? A life where you know the gifts and talents that He gave you and you make it your life's mission to use them. A life full of possibility, where anything can happen. A life that doesn't look like anyone else's because it's your unique walk with God, yielded to His will.

God has so much more for us if we open ourselves up to the full abundant life He has planned for us. There are so many possibilities.

Let's think about this- what did Jesus really have in mind when he offered us an abundant life? There is a river of life within us waiting to flow out to the world. God has so much more for us than a routine, mundane life. He wants to partner with us so that His goodness flows from our lives.

The amplified Bible says,

> *He who believes in Me [who cleaves to and trusts in and relies on Me] as the Scripture has said, From his innermost being shall flow [continuously] springs and rivers of living water.*
> *John 7:38 AMP*

Living water! Stagnant water is not living water.

Our lives aren't meant to be stagnant, with each day looking a lot like the last, nor are we meant to fill our lives with entertainment.

We are meant to live with purpose. The abundant life is one where we are not held back by fear or expectations. It's a life where we take risks, try new things, rely on God and see him move in our lives. When we partner with him and let him lead us, then the river of life flows through us out to the world and changes it. Christians were meant to impact the world. Consider this,

"Your lives light up the world. Let others see your light from a distance, for how can you hide a city that stands on a hilltop? And who would light a lamp and then hide it in an obscure place? Instead, it's placed where everyone in the house can benefit from its light. So don't hide your light! Let it shine brightly before others, so that the commendable things you do will shine as light upon them, and then they will give their praise to your Father in heaven." Matthew 5:14-16, Passion Translation

If you want that abundant life that God has for you, for the river to flow out of you, keep reading. If you want your light to inspire others to follow Jesus, join me on this journey. If you have secretly been desiring more out of your life and your walk with Jesus, then this book is for you. If you are tired of going through the motions of Christianity and desire to live fully in what He has planned for you, then keep reading. If you have been living in fear for way too long and want to step out of fear and into a faith filled journey toward the best that He has planned for you then dive in and let's see where this might take you.

Anything is possible. Your potential is infinite. It will always increase if you keep expanding and growing. By God's great design there is greatness inside you. Weren't you made in His image? How can you be created in the image of a great God and not carry seeds of greatness inside you? There is greatness in you.

God has placed a desire in my heart to inspire His people to embrace that greatness and move into a new season with Him where more of us embrace the full abundant life that we can have with Him and partner with Him to live it. So many of us live in fear and that fear reduces our lives into merely going through the motions of life and never fully realize what God has planned for us.

What types of fear do we go through? We are afraid of what people will think, so we conform. We do what everyone else is doing. We are afraid we don't have the time or money to pursue all that God has for us. We are afraid the people we love won't understand or support what we want to do. We are afraid we aren't good enough or talented enough to do it. We are afraid to fail so we never even try. We fear the unknown, so we settle for what is known and what is easy. We fear that the cost is too high, the sacrifice to great.

I believe this breaks God's heart. He sees the fullness of the abundant life we could be living if we stepped out of fear and he sees the limitations that we have built like a stone wall around our lives. He also sees the people we could impact with the gifts He has given us. He gave us those gifts for a specific reason and he knows all the good we could spread in the world if we chose to use those gifts. He knows the joy we would feel if we stepped into the light and let ourselves shine. He grieves for the abundant life we could be living. He desires to knock down those walls and set us free! He wants to knock those walls of fear and doubt. The walls of shame that make us feel like we aren't good enough. The walls of small thinking and impossibility. What would it feel like to tear down those walls and be free to believe that God has something great planned for us to do? **How would it feel to be truly free to live the life that we are meant to live?**

So, how 'bout it? Let's take a few swings with our spiritual sledgehammer and begin the process of tearing down those walls!

— *chapter 1* —

THE DAY THAT CHANGED EVERYTHING

IT'S ETCHED IN my memory like it happened yesterday, not every moment of that day, but the moment I got the call.

In many ways that day was like any other. I woke up early to read and pray before preparing myself and my children for the day. We got ready and ate our breakfast before driving to school. I dropped them off and listened to a great podcast on the way to my office. When I arrived at the office, there was a lot to do. Our office was being audited in a few days, so we were checking our files and making sure everything was in order. The morning was flying by when - suddenly - I was interrupted.

I got the call I had been dreading.

What I always feared has happened to me. What I dreaded has come true. Job 3:25 NLT

It was bad news. Kathy, my eldest sister, was in the hospital. Now this alone wasn't what rocked my world, she had cancer after all. A few trips to the hospital were to be expected. She had been diagnosed with lung cancer 6 months earlier. Just 6 months previous, we had danced at our cousin's wedding and stayed up way too late, laughing and talking. What rocked my world was what came next, she'd been admitted to the palliative care unit. In this hospital, that is where you go when they have stopped fighting the cancer and have determined that you will soon pass away. They focus moves to easing the pain not treatment.

I closed my office door and leaned against it, tears running down my face as I slid down to the floor. How could this be happening? How could I lose my sister? How could I face saying goodbye? Why hadn't God answered our many prayers and healed her?

As I drove the 3 long hours to the city where she lived, I cried out to God to save her. The 300 kilometres felt like 800 kilometres. I just wanted to be there, to see her, and talk to her. I prayed over and over, declaring the goodness and power of my God to heal. My God that saves, who is more than able to speak to every cancer cell in her body and cast them into the pit of hell. I had seen my God move and miraculously heal so I knew a miracle was possible. I prayed for the spirit of the Lord to invade her hospital room and make her well. When I couldn't pray, I sang songs of worship, letting them sooth my broken soul. I recited every verse that I knew from memory like Psalm 91 - He that dwells in the shelter of the Most High will find rest in the shadow of the Almighty.

When I arrived at the hospital, I was shocked at what I saw, even though I had visited her just a few weeks earlier. She was so thin. How could this happen so fast? She struggled to breathe and the pain was so bad. The drugs they gave her took the pain away but also changed her. She wasn't herself and she hated it. She tried not to take them and when she could manage it, she would say something witty and make us laugh.

You don't really ever think about what would go through your mind if you knew it was your last days. What would be important? What would you want said and done? In the midst of the pain and the struggle to breathe, Kathy was preparing. Preparing to say goodbye to all of us. She comforted us, held us in her arms. She told us we would be ok. She prepared her children, said everything that could be said. She recorded messages for the grandchildren she wouldn't see grow up. She wanted them to know what was special about them and how much she had loved them. She was calm and strong like she always was in a crisis. She had a peaceful acceptance of her fate like the old hymn says "It is well with my soul."

She was so strong, taking over, planning, taking care of us, when we should have been taking care of her.

She had a list of things we would need to do after and made sure I wrote them down. Like she was planning one of her perfect family gatherings. She was like that, she thought of the details, all the little things that I always miss. I admired that about her. She remembered the practical things like shutting down her Facebook. She chose the music for her funeral. She talked about the kind of flowers she wanted. Live, planted flowers not cut flowers that would fade quickly and die. How could we bear to watch flowers die, too? No, she wanted it to reflect life, not death. What a beautiful gift that was for all of us. We all took some of these flowers home with us and thought of her each time we saw them. It was all so surreal. Was I really talking to my beloved sister about planning her funeral that was likely just days away? I wondered if this was really the most important conversation to be having now. Upon reflection, I realize now that the to-do list gave her some sense of control over a situation in which she had no control. Her life was ending, she couldn't change that but she could plan one last beautiful event where we would say goodbye. She could help create the perfect gathering one last time. She had a vision for it, how it would reflect who she was and what was important to her. Her daughter caught the vision and carried out the plan flawlessly. It was amazing how that gave us so much comfort, to see how God had placed the same gifts and talents in her daughter. We knew we hadn't lost her completely. We would forever see glimpses of our Kathy reflected in her children.

How do you say goodbye to someone you love so much? Someone who loved you and understood you like only a sister could. She had this way of making you feel so loved and understood even though I am sure she often didn't feel that way. With Kathy, I felt safe, like I could be me and could still be loved. I look back at that time and wonder why I didn't say more. Why didn't I express how much I loved her more eloquently and fully? I sometimes felt like the words just weren't enough or maybe they just wouldn't come. Maybe I couldn't fully accept that this was the end. When you rehearse these things in your mind, imagining what you would say to someone you love on their deathbed, it seems like there should be a lot to say. We see scenes in TV shows or movies, and they always say these beautiful things, but when it is real, it isn't like that. At least it wasn't for me. The grief got in the way. Like a tidal wave it came and washed all the words away. I often wish I would have said more. God has given me peace about this though. Maybe God showed her. I imagine this huge screen in heaven where God shows you the difference you have made in the world, what you meant to the people you love. I imagine Kathy watching the movie of her life and knowing how important and loved she really was.

– *chapter 2* –

BECOMING A SISTER

I WAS BORN into my family as the fourth daughter; the last attempt to have a son in an era when a son meant your family name continued and was your legacy. To say my dad was disappointed would be the understatement of the century which sent me on a quest to be "Daddy's little girl" and be as good as any son. Over the years, my dad and I had a lot of conversations about why a son was so important and I argued strongly that a daughter could be all that a son could be. I soon realized that I was not going to change his mind. A son could take over his trucking company. A son would carry on the Hansen name. He really couldn't see his daughter running his trucking company and knew she would one day marry and change her name. I may have believed that I could do anything a boy could do and maybe even do it better, but my dear father couldn't see it. Now don't take this the wrong way, our father loved us and is such a strong stable, positive presence in our lives. I am incredibly grateful to call him "my favourite Dad". It did, however, mean that I wanted to prove I was good enough and wanted to prove he didn't need a son. This created a drive and ambition in me that has served me well.

Being the fourth daughter meant I had 3 big sisters. I wanted to be like all my sisters. I wished I was as pretty as they were. I wanted to dress how they dressed, and act how they acted. In some ways, this made me grow up too fast. By the time I was 10, I was wearing makeup and always had a crush on a boy. My eldest sister, Kathy, was 10 years older than me, so you'd think we'd have very little in common but in fact the age gap made us closer. We were always in completely different stages so perhaps there was less competition and jealousy, I'm not exactly sure but she was my safe haven, someone I could relax and be myself with. It wasn't perfect; don't get me wrong. She could react quickly and get crazy emotional. I remember one time when Mom left her in charge one evening and we all were not listening to her. She was so frustrated. Of course, that made it even more fun for us and my rebellion escalated. I am not sure exactly what I did that made her so mad but at one point she hit me across the face with a leather belt. I don't remember if it really hurt but I was just SO shocked and hid in my room until Mom came home. This is the one time that I remember us fighting. We had a really positive relationship. She told me how much she loved having a baby sister when she was 10 years old. A baby to cuddle and play with whenever you want. I am sure she was a big help to my mom in the days where every household chore was done manually, and laundry was a full day chore morning to night. I mean just think, cloth diapers and no electric washing machine? That is just crazy!

We didn't live together long though, when I was 8 years old and she was just 17, she wanted to get married. This was a crazy time for our family. My parents were not happy about their 17-year-old daughter, who hadn't finished high school yet, getting married. They weren't sure he was the right man for her, and they weren't sure why they were rushing into it. They did all they could to talk her out of it and even had my grandma and uncles try to change her mind. My dad even offered to send her to Ontario to live with my uncle if she was looking for a way out. She didn't take it. They decided to get married without my parents blessing on her 18th birthday when they wouldn't need their parents' permission. My parents weren't invited and none of us attended. It was just the two of them and two witnesses. My mom cried all day that day. It was a weekday and I remember going to school knowing my sister was getting married. It did not seem right. It was difficult for all of us and it could have torn our family apart but even though they were terribly hurt by this decision, they chose to forgive. My dad and her husband even became good friends over the years. Their marriage was tumultuous from the start. A roller coaster of sweet tender moments and out of control fights. There are certain personalities that just aren't good together. There were times where they truly brought the worst out of each other.

A few years later, she was pregnant and we were all so excited. I was over the moon excited about becoming an aunty. In her 6th or 7th month they realized a little too late that she had preeclampsia. This is a condition where the mother's blood pressure gets dangerously high and she starts retaining large amounts of fluid. Kathy was typically a small, thin person but in her pregnancy, she gained huge amounts of weight because of the fluid. She was carrying a 2 lb baby but gained 60+ lbs! They realized the baby wasn't getting the nutrition it needed and so she was admitted to the Calgary Foothills Hospital. She was only in her 7th month of the pregnancy and she went into labour. The rest of us were on vacation out of the country at the time. We weren't expecting her to deliver so early. I can't imagine what that was like for her. She was so young and she must have been so scared. Her parents and her sisters were 1000s of miles away as she was going through a life altering event. She had her baby, born prematurely at 2.5 lbs. A tiny baby girl whom they named Pamela.

She was so tiny that head to toe she could fit in the palm of her dad's hand. A fighter from the very start. The doctors were surprised that her lungs were already developed enough to supply her body with the oxygen she needed. That was a great blessing. Pam spent 2 months in the Foothills hospital before she came home. I remember Kathy and her husband driving back and forth to Calgary over those 2 months to be with her.

Pamela seemed to be doing well in her first year but then started missing many of her milestones. She didn't learn to crawl or walk until much later than most children. She would also get so sick if she caught a cold and would often end up in the hospital. It wasn't until she was about 2 years old that they found out that Pam was deprived oxygen during the birth and had cerebral palsy. This was all very overwhelming for Kathy. Raising a child is challenging as it is but raising a child with disabilities is even more stressful and put a lot of strain on an already difficult marriage.

I spent a lot of time in Kathy's home during these years and learned a lot about marriage and relationships as a result. Both Kathy and her husband were good people, I believe they loved each other but just weren't good together. Sometimes love itself isn't enough. I have no doubt that Kathy and her husband had love for each other. It is important to think about that when choosing a partner. Choose someone you love that brings out the best in you, someone that makes you want to be better and supports your growth. Choose someone that is willing to change and grow too. Is the person willing to ask for help if things aren't going well? Married people often bring a lot of pain and hurt from the past into their marriages and if that pain isn't dealt with it can poison the marriage. We all have had things happen in the past that have hurt us and changed us and it can hinder us from having healthy relationships if we don't heal that pain.

I have seen it in myself. I will overreact to something that happens and I will realize my reaction isn't about what is presently happening, it's actually about what has happened in the past. Our past influences our future if we allow it to.

I spent a lot of years full of anger and unforgiveness towards Kathy's husband. Recently, God told me to forgive him. Am I so perfect that I have the right to judge another? Definitely not! Now I can see the good in him. I see how he helps out his children, trying to make their lives easier as they raise their families. I see how dedicated he is to Pam and how patient he is with her. He makes great effort to stay connected to my father visiting him in the seniors home that he lives in. There are many who don't make that effort. He's dedicated to his own parents too, helping them out in their old age. You see, unforgiveness can blind us and distort how we see people. I used to only see his faults. No, he isn't perfect but then none of us are, are we?

Kathy had 2 more children over the next 4 or 5 years. She struggled to handle it all and all three of us sisters helped a lot. I was a very willing helper and felt like the luckiest 10-year-old ever to become an aunty so early in life. Now I know that Kathy thought I was helping her out and often thought it was a burden on me. The fact is it helped me too. That was a particularly low time in my life where I felt like an outsider everywhere else except in her home. That was where I was accepted, loved, and needed. It was the absolute highlight of that period in my life. Those pre-teen and teen years are so uncertain and so filled with self-doubt. Her home was the one place I felt safe and accepted. It built my self-worth and self-esteem. I will never forget how I felt when I walked through her door and was greeted with the most enthusiastic "Aunty Arly!" and her 2 girls (and later her son) would run across the room arms wide open. Suddenly it didn't matter that I didn't fit in anywhere else.

The challenges and obstacles we face carry with them seeds of great blessing and benefit. Genesis 50:20 says that what was meant to harm Joseph, God used for good. Joseph was sold into slavery, imprisoned, and accused of attempted rape. Joseph's brothers meant to harm him and God used it to promote Joseph into a position of high authority. It didn't happen right away but over years God used it to promote Joseph, which ultimately saved Joseph's entire family, including those vindictive brothers! The challenges and obstacles made Joseph a better, stronger man, one capable of leading the nation.

We live in a broken world; it isn't what God meant for it to be. **But God takes what challenges us and hurts us and wants to use it for good.** For our good and for the good of others. To help us encourage others or to give someone purpose or belonging and so much more. Kathy's marriage and family life was so hard. If it wasn't so hard, she wouldn't have needed us so much. If she hadn't needed me, I would have missed out on one of the most defining and rewarding experiences of my life. I honestly could have slipped down a very destructive road at that time as well. **Helping her saved me!** Now don't get me wrong, I wish that Kathy's life had been easier, I wish she had more joy and less struggle in those years, and I am quite certain God wished the same for her. Our free will takes us through challenges that He never would have planned for us but regardless of our mistakes, God can and will use those detours and challenges for good. That is His promise!

Your life may not look exactly how you hoped it would be. Maybe your marriage has failed or looks like it is heading that way. Maybe a child is making bad decisions and you are trying to figure out what went wrong. Maybe you sacrificed everything for your children and now that they are grown, they've estranged themselves from you. You had this picture-perfect idea of what parenthood was going to be and your child was born with a disability. Maybe you invested everything you had in a business idea and your business has failed. It has changed everything. This was not what you expected; life didn't turn out how you imagined. How do you live abundantly now despite all these failures and setbacks? I believe that despite all that has gone wrong, God still has a great plan for you. It may look different than what you expected but it can still be great.

In Jeremiah 29, the Lord encouraged his people. They had been exiled and were in Babylon. It was not what they had planned nor wanted. God's people didn't listen to God and they were living with those consequences. They were exiled from their beautiful homeland and now living as foreigners in Babylon. I assume they were feeling a little uncertain about their future and their place in a foreign land. God encouraged them through Jeremiah. He sent Jeremiah to tell them to settle there. To embrace life in Babylon, not resist it,

> *"Build houses and settle down; plant gardens and eat what they produce. Marry and have sons and daughters; find wives for your sons and give your daughters in marriage, so that they too may have sons and daughters. Increase in number there; do not decrease. Also, seek the peace and prosperity of the city to which I have carried you into exile. Pray to the LORD for it, because if it prospers, you too will prosper." Jeremiah 29:5-7 NIV*

They hadn't planned to be exiled; life had not turned out the way they thought it would. They could have chosen to be angry and bitter about it or to thrive and prosper. **I believe if you seek the will of God for your life in this season, you can thrive too.** If you start believing that you can prosper, even though life has taken you places you didn't plan to go, then God can use it for good. God can turn your hurt, disappointments, and failures into a great testimony if you will partner with Him and follow the plan that He has for you now. Joseph allowed God to use him even when he was imprisoned. He could have been angry and bitter about his imprisonment and stopped listening to God. Instead, he waited and prepared himself for the day that God would use it for good. He listened to God and believed in His future. God had shown him in a dream, when he was a child, that he would rule and have great influence. Then he was imprisoned, how could that dream come to pass? Joseph knew God would find a way and trusted him. When God opened the door, Joseph obeyed, followed God and was promoted into the palace.

We have all had disappointments and failures and so often we allow them to hold us back and define us. **God doesn't define us by our failures; he never allows our past to define our future.** Instead, he uses our past to show others what is possible if we believe we can prosper even when we fail or face disappointment. Do not allow the negative experiences to create so much fear and doubt that you stop believing that God has a plan for you. There are no failures and no disappointments that are too big for God to overcome. The enemy wants you to believe it is hopeless, he wants you to feel powerless, but God wants to empower you to keep going. He wants you to prosper despite all that you have gone through. The enemy uses our shame and doubt to stop us. If he can make us believe that we don't deserve a second chance and that nothing ever works out for us, then he can stop us from being used by God. He can stop the plans God has for us. **All the failure, all the disappointment will only make your testimony of what God has done better!**

This book is about finding and honouring those seeds of blessings in the midst of great trial and loss. It is about allowing what is devastating to change and improve you and draw you deeper into your God-given purpose. You can allow the challenges and tough times to make you bitter or you can allow it to make you better. It's up to you. God wants to use it for good. He wants to turn your test into a testimony! It's about changing your perspective and changing what you focus on when you think about the loss or trial you have been through.

> *They triumphed over him by the blood of the Lamb <u>and by the word of their testimony</u>; they did not love their lives so much as to shrink from death. Revelation 12:11 NIV*

So, let's start there. Write down a few challenges or difficult, painful experiences that you have walked through and start looking for the seeds of blessing that were sown in those experiences. Who else was impacted? Who else was given the chance to serve or help because of your experience? Who was given new purpose? Who was given the opportunity to love unconditionally? How did it change your perspective or theirs? How did it change you? **Take a moment RIGHT NOW to journal about that.** Don't wait or you won't do it. Seriously. Write it down right now and honour what God did through you and in you. There are seeds of blessing sprinkled among the challenges, I am sure of it. **If you can honour what God did through the challenge and be grateful despite the disappointment it opens the door for God to move in your life.**

> *"Always be joyful. Never stop praying. Be thankful in all circumstances, for this is God's will for you who belong to Christ Jesus." Thessalonians 5:16-18 NLT*

Develop a habit of looking for the seeds of blessing no matter what happens. God is working in your life, even through the trials. We may not always see it, but he is there, and he is using it for good. Choose to believe that today!

— chapter 3 —

THE GREAT LOSS

IT WAS OCTOBER 2016 and I was at my office late one evening when my other sister, Wanda, sent me a text message asking me to call her. I dialed her number before I pulled out of the parking lot, thinking the drive home would be the perfect time to chat. I was surprised when she told me to call her back when I got home. I got this uneasy feeling in the pit of my stomach. Something was wrong! My mind started racing and I imagined all sorts of terrible things. It was a long 20-minute drive home.

When I arrived safely home, I braced myself, and called her back. "Kathy has cancer and it's in stage 4." I wasn't prepared to hear those words at all. I actually didn't know what stage 4 meant and oh how I wish I could go back to the innocence of that moment. I wish I still didn't know what Stage 4 cancer meant. Now, I know it means the chances of survival are low and there is no viable way to beat it. That day changed everything about how I see the world. There was now a clear line - before Kathy had cancer and after Kathy got cancer. Two distinct times and two radically different perspectives.

The next 6 months were an emotional roller coaster as we tried to support her through this battle. We cried so many tears and prayed so many prayers. We encouraged her with prayer, scripture, and endless text messages. She fought valiantly against it but on April 27, 2017 she lost the fight against cancer and went home to be with Jesus. It's hard to believe; it all happened so fast. She literally went from riding her horse around the prairie, so vibrant and full of life, to her death bed in mere months.

The will to live is so strong. When the doctors had no hope, and no treatment options, she found a place in Mexico with alternative treatment, and spent several weeks there. When she returned home she found practitioners here that offered some of the same treatments. She wanted to beat the cancer; she tried everything. We had so much hope that something would work or God would miraculously heal her. We honestly did not believe she would die, that was not a thought we allowed ourselves to have. I still wonder if that was a good way to think or not? If I had accepted that she was going to die, would I have spent more time with her? Yes, I definitely would have but is it better to accept our fate or live with hope? I think I would choose hope again if faced with the same situation. What if there was a treatment that helped? What if God moved His mighty hand and healed her?

There are regrets though, deep heart wrenching regrets. This may be the most difficult part of the book to write but also the most important. If it helps one person make different decisions in a time like this then it is worth it. If one person can avoid the regret I have then it is worth it. If one person can forgive themselves for making the same mistakes then it is also worth it. I regret not spending more time with Kathy during those 6 months. She did push me away; avoiding my phone calls, and being busy with treatments to try to get better, but I wish I had shown up anyway. I wish I had just shown up on her doorstep instead of waiting for the call back or the invite. I am not exactly sure why she withdrew from me in that time. I will never know. But fighting cancer can do a lot to our emotions; I can't even begin to understand. I also regret the decision I had made on her last day. Even though I had spent many days that week at the hospital with her, I could not bring myself to go to the hospital to be there that final day. I just couldn't do it. I should have been stronger for her, for her children, for my parents. It seems like Kathy knew somehow that I wouldn't be there. When I left the hospital for the last time she said goodbye like it was the last time. She asked me to take care of Pam and then said "I hate goodbyes." I am working on forgiving myself, but haven't quite got there yet. I think God is going to have to help me with that one. I have very deep regret. I hope my confessions make a difference. I hope it will cause someone to be stronger than I was when someone they love goes through a struggle like this. If someone you know is ill and shutting you out, try harder. Don't let yourself feel rejected by it, just know that they are facing their worst fears and feeling so many emotions. Do whatever you can to be there.

Those moments in the last few weeks of her fight taught me a lot about life. It taught me the value of a day; a day spent with someone you love. It taught me the value of a conversation. It revealed the value of our words, of expressing to people what they mean to us. I now know the value of truly knowing someone and what is important to them, the value of taking time to ask the ones I love questions so that I can learn who they are, what they love, their dreams, and regrets. What makes them feel alive. It taught me the value of a sentence; the value of speaking my truth even when I am filled with insecurity and doubt. It taught me the value of looking someone in the eyes and not saying anything at all. Two hearts connecting without any words at all. I realized the value of a hug when it was the very last one this side of eternity.

To say I miss her doesn't quite capture the ache in my heart whenever I realize I can't talk to her anymore. There were moments like the one a few months after she passed. I had a problem and the first person I thought to call was Kathy. I picked up my phone, but then remembered she wasn't there to call. It hurts to realize that I will never feel her arms embrace me again. Kathy gave great hugs, real hugs; the kind of hug that told you that she cared and wasn't just going through the motions. I miss her laugh - she had our grandma's laugh - kind of a chuckle but a little more enthusiastic than a chuckle. Knowing I will never see her excitement over some new idea again, brings pain. She always had a new idea and she would get so excited.

In the months after I said goodbye to my beloved sister, there was rarely a day that I didn't cry. I wondered, how can I move on and allow this loss to move me forward instead of holding me back? It's so hard to imagine how much something like this changes you until you experience it, but I hope my story will inspire you to live fuller, richer, more purposeful lives without ever having to suffer such a great loss. If you have already experienced such a loss, I hope this book encourages you to keep living your best life. I hope it helps you move out of bitterness and anger. I hope it helps you embrace the abundant life, the one God has perfectly planned for you. There are no guarantees in this life. You don't know how long you have. Losing my 52-year-old sister when I was 42 years old has helped me understand that life truly is incredibly short. I lost my beautiful sister. Everything about it seems wrong and unjust. I could let those feelings grow roots until I am angry and bitter but I've chosen another way. Instead, I've decided to live my life to the fullest in her memory. Life is short and I am going to squeeze every last drop of joy out of it! I want to challenge you to do the same! I believe that when we get to the gates of heaven and meet our God, he will show us the good we have done in the world and how we had made an impact. I also believe he will show us what we could have done if we had followed his will and his plan for us. What could have happened if we had acted in faith instead of fear. I hope those two movies are close to the same, I pray they aren't two radically different stories. I hope this for me, and I hope this for YOU. **If this book inspires just one person to live a life that is fuller, more joyful, and closer to what God has planned then it has done what it is supposed to do.**

— *chapter 4* —

IT'S OKAY TO INCONVENIENCE PEOPLE… PEOPLE THAT YOU LOVE

WE HAVE A saying in my business "It's okay to inconvenience people when it's for their own good." It helps us to stop worrying about what other people think and focus more on the good we can bring into their lives with the help that we offer. I've realized that we need to stop worrying about inconveniencing those we love as well. We miss out on so many moments because we are focused on convenience, whether it be our own or someone else's.

Have you ever been driving through a town or city and thought, "I should pop in on so and so on my way through town," but then you talk yourself out of it? You convince yourself that you shouldn't drop in unannounced or on short notice, it might be inconvenient, they might be busy. Maybe it'll stress them out and they'll feel obligated to feed you. Why upset someone's well thought out schedule? Besides, you really don't have that much time anyway and it is a little out of your way. Does any of this sound familiar?

So now, consider this question - if you knew that you may

only have 6 or 12 months left with that person, would you worry about all those little inconveniences? Would you make the time to fit the visit in? If the answer is "Yes," then I encourage you to drop in unannounced or with short notice. **We all worry so much about the little things, how clean our house is, whipping up the perfect meal, or inconveniencing someone a little, and as a result we miss out.** We miss out on connecting with someone, having a great conversation, or finding out a little more about the people we care about. **They seem like the little things in life but they are actually the big things. The most important things.**

If you think about it, how well do you actually know the most important people in your life? Do you know their hopes and dreams? Do you know what they are passionate about? What they love to do or wish they could do? I am thankful for the conversations my sister and I did have. She was a deep thinker, always contemplating life, so we would have these deep conversations. I miss those conversations and I wish we would have had more.

For this to happen though, **we are going to have to care less about perfection and more about connection.** Our generation isn't very good at this anymore. We have to pre-plan everything and make everything perfect before we invite anyone over. So, over the years, we have fewer guests, fewer friends and less and less connection with those we care about. We become more and more isolated. Growing up it was very different in my family. My parents were always connecting with friends or family. I can remember my mom throwing a roast beef in the oven with some potatoes and heading off to church. My dad would then find someone available to come over for dinner after church. It wasn't pre-planned six weeks in advance. My mom didn't spend hours and hours preparing something elaborate. We all pitched in when we got home and served a great meal. I cut the pickles and made the gravy. We even used the good china and fancy silverware! It wasn't just in a cabinet on display. Our home was filled with great conversation and our family was connected. It felt like we were part of a community. That community is still a great source of strength and support for my parents today. I can't really imagine how my parents would have survived the last few years without that community.

My sister and I lived in different cities that are about a 3-hour drive away from each other. We didn't see each other often enough. My city has the largest airport in the area and several times a year my sister would fly out of my city and stay in a hotel near the airport either on the way out or on the way home from her trips. I'm sure she didn't want to inconvenience me - you know - dirty the sheets on my spare bed, wake up my babies at 5 am when she needed to catch her flight, and ask me to drive her across town. On this side of losing her, I am wishing she would have. I also didn't make the effort to visit her enough. We were busy, busy working and running our children to activities. I wish I had made more effort. How many conversations and moments were missed? Perhaps we would have been closer those last few years, perhaps my boys would have known their aunty a little better. We always assume we will have more time, don't we? We had plans for the summer after she passed away. A road trip to South Dakota for our family reunion. A visit to her cabin with my boys. Plans that never happened. We tell ourselves we can visit next month, or next summer or next year. What if you don't have the chance next summer or next year?

I am giving you permission!! Go ahead and inconvenience someone you love this week or this month, and then make a habit of it! Go ahead, call last minute; drop in unannounced; invite someone over! All in the name of getting one more precious moment with them. AND for those of you on the receiving end of it, I give you permission to order pizza for your surprise guests or throw some frozen burgers on the BBQ. I think about this every time I'm in the freezer section of my grocery store. I do the mental check "Do I have the frozen burgers in the freezer just in case someone pops in?" If I don't, I grab a box and a bag of buns. I am ready. Just keep it simple and enjoy the conversation. I am guessing one day it will become a treasured memory! And remember it is okay to inconvenience people when it's someone you love.

– *chapter 5* –

YOU ARE LOVED!
NOW BELIEVE IT!

IF I TOLD you that your family and friends love you more than you think they do, would you believe it? Probably not. Instead, you think of the moments that you felt rejected, ignored or judged by them. You feel so misunderstood and that causes you to hide your real amazing self from those you love in an effort to self-protect. You are afraid your authentic self will be judged and rejected so you hide that person away. It's a vicious cycle. You hide your awesomeness from everyone but occasionally it slips out and they don't really know how to react. This isn't the person they typically see so they really aren't sure what to do with you. You interpret that reaction (or lack of reaction) as judgement and push down all your awesomeness again. Then the pattern starts all over again until you decide that there are very few people you can share your true self with and you feel more alone every day. You make up this new person that's "acceptable" but not real and you walk around pretending that's who you are. This acceptable version of you is like you but a less passionate and less creative version of you. It's the price we pay to fit in and belong. It is what you think you need to do to belong and be accepted. As a result, the world misses out on the greatness that is inside you and is dying to get out. It's like a gold mine deep below the surface of the earth that's never discovered. Very valuable and could do so much for so many but it's never discovered. It's heart breaking.

Before Kathy was diagnosed with cancer, I believe she felt so misunderstood and judged by her family that she really didn't want to spend much time with us. Honestly, I don't blame her for that, most of us didn't really "get" her most of the time. We were always trying to figure out why she did the things she did and it never really made much sense to us. I think she was a sensitive, emotional person with so much creativity running through her veins that her brain was always thinking of something new and amazing to do. She went through these cycles of really high excitement about a new idea to really low times when she wasn't using her creativity. We were never sure who we were going to encounter - the excited Kathy or the depressed Kathy. Being highly sensitive, she sensed all of that and as a result felt so misunderstood.

Maybe you can relate to that feeling? Do you struggle to feel like you belong? Certain life experiences can make you feel alone and misunderstood. For as long as I can remember this has been something I have battled with. Take for example the relationship between my three sisters and I. The older three were all just a few years apart and went through all the ages and stages relatively close together. Being the youngest and a bit of an afterthought left this gap between them and I. When they were raising children; I was still in high school and college. When I had young children, theirs were moving out. Now, my children are teenagers, and they are having grandchildren. I have always been just far enough behind to have less in common with them. At times, feeling like I belong in this family has been fleeting. There are many reasons people can feel like they don't belong.

It can be because their family didn't look like everyone else's growing up or they came from another culture. It is so easy to focus on what makes us different when the reality is we are all more similar than we realize. Maybe we are dealing with different challenges and situations but most of us have similar insecurities. We wonder if we fit in and if people really care. We wonder if we are good enough, smart enough, or funny enough to be loved and accepted. We question if they really knew us, the real us, would we still fit in and be accepted?

What if we could start to embrace each other's differences and celebrate them? Maybe the answer is to stop wanting everyone to think like us and live like us. Perhaps it is our differences that can make us better. God made all of us to be unique and different. It is hard to wrap our head around that since there are billions of people on this planet and our limited human minds struggle to see how it is possible that we are all so unique. God's design is for all of us to be unique and different. Yet we spend so much time trying to be like everyone else. This must be heart-breaking to God. If he wanted us to be like everyone else, he would have made us all the same.

Psalm 139:13-18 says it beautifully,

For you created my inmost being;
you knit me together in my mother's womb.
I praise you because I am fearfully and wonderfully made;
your works are wonderful,
I know that full well.
My frame was not hidden from you
when I was made in the secret place,
when I was woven together in the depths of the earth.
Your eyes saw my unformed body;
all the days ordained for me were written in your book

before one of them came to be.
How precious to me are your thoughts, God!
How vast is the sum of them!
Were I to count them, they would outnumber the grains of sand—when I awake, I am still with you. - NIV

Who God made you to be is wonderful. No matter the circumstances of your birth, you were fearfully and wonderfully made. Your earthly parents may not have planned you, but your heavenly father did. There are no surprises to our God. Your authentic self is who God really wants you to be. When we start to accept that maybe we can start to accept others. What if we could be more like David and treasure the thoughts that God has about us? When we start to do that maybe it would lead us to treasure the thoughts that God has about others. That would lead to real acceptance and love.

How can we embrace our differences and be more accepting of who people really are? Here are a few things I am trying to practice. I say practice because I am not perfect at it but I am trying to practice until it feels more reflexive and natural for me.

1. Stop trying to understand people.

Now I know that might be the opposite of what you were expecting. Stay with me to the end on this one, I think it will shift your perspective. I'm not sure it serves anyone to try to understand them. It is so difficult. We don't see the world through their lenses. We don't have their perspective and we really can't. They have had different experiences and they also have unique personalities. They have different emotions and triggers. What hurts one person, may have no impact on another. It's likely they've also been hurt or had trauma that we have never experienced and it has changed how they see the world and it drives their decisions. These experiences can be like a different lens. Have you ever tried on someone else's glasses and tried to see? It is difficult, isn't it? That's a lot like trying to understand why people do the things they do. Besides, rarely do people share enough about themselves for you to even begin to understand them. If they are vulnerable enough to share anything at all, they share a tiny little part of their story and then you THINK that you understand them. The truth is, you don't know enough to really understand. They give you a glimpse and you think you see the whole picture. Perhaps your job isn't to understand them but just to LOVE them, all of them. The amazing parts and the crazy parts! Let's face it, we ALL have both, don't we? The best relationships I have are the relationships where we both accept ALL of each other. The good, the great and the crazy! The great thing that happens when you do this is that the crazy parts don't bother you quite as much. It actually becomes endearing and you begin to love that about them.

Who do you need to stop trying to understand and just love and accept unconditionally? Pray about this. God will show you how to love that person. All of them. Ask God to help you love the good things and the things that drive you crazy. Ask God to open your eyes to the greatness and uniqueness that He placed in that person. Start praying for that person. Pray into their purpose and the plans of God in their life. Watch how your relationship with that person changes and flourishes.

2. Stop trying to change the people you love.

People seldom change because we want them to. I have even heard it said that people can't change. That's not true, people can change but they really need to want to. It's completely up to them. No amount of lecturing (I prefer to call it 'giving advice') discussing, or analysing is going to inspire anyone to change! If Kathy was here to agree with me, I am pretty sure she would say an enthusiastic "Amen, sister!" Oh, how I tried to change her. Now I called it "helping her". I tried to help her see life in a different way, encouraging her to make decisions differently and it pushed her away. Please hear me when I say this. It pushed her away. My intentions were good, I wanted her to be happy and live life to the fullest. I wonder now, though, what if I had just focused on her amazing talents and gifts, the way I did after her diagnosis? The way we all did after her diagnosis. I find it fascinating that after her diagnosis, her greatness suddenly became so obvious to all of us. It was all we could see. It was like new light was shining on all that made her unique and beautiful. When faced with the possibility of losing her, all we could see was the potential and possibility of who God made her to be. Perhaps that kind of acceptance pre-cancer would have made her more comfortable in who she really was? Perhaps she would have been more aware of who God created her to be? At the very least, she would have known without a shadow of doubt how treasured and loved she was. So, you are off the hook, you don't need to change anyone! Whew what a relief, it is a hard enough job trying to change yourself, you really don't need to take on anyone else.

Who do you need to stop trying to change? Change is an inside job; it is between God and that person. Ask God to show you who He created that person to be and then start encouraging that person. Not with the intention of changing them, but in an effort to build them up and strengthen their identity of who they were made to be. I have had people in my life see the potential in me far before it was obvious to me. When they encouraged me, I knew they were speaking the truth. It resonated deeply in my heart. It clarified the purpose that God has for my life and strengthened my resolve to live in that purpose. So just as 1 Thessalonians 5:11 reminds us to *"encourage one another and build each other up"* make it your focus to find the gifts and blessings in others and have the courage to tell them. It is perfectly okay to tell them more than once. They may need to be reminded as it is easy to forget. It is so easy to remember our shortcomings and faults, isn't it? Just as it is easy to see the faults of others. It takes purposeful effort to stay focused on what it good and wonderful in ourselves and others. It will be worth the effort though because as you do you will see more of their God given greatness come shining through. So let's stop trying to change people and instead look for what is good and wonderful and leave the rest to God.

3. Listen more and talk less.

I have a friend who is an amazing listener. When there is something, I'm working out in my life, she is an amazing sounding board. She'll listen to it all and then say something profound like,

"It sounds like you are feeling _____."

I've realized that she doesn't listen to give advice (like someone else I know really well…) She really listens, not so she can respond with something profound, but she just listens. She listens for the feelings in the story and then reflects it back to me and I feel so understood and accepted. So relieved. Then something amazing happens! I can let go of whatever feeling is holding me hostage and move on. It is amazing!

So, my challenge for you is to try that with someone you love the next time they are venting or struggling with something and watch what happens. Just listen, no interrupting and NO advice-giving. Try to pinpoint the feeling behind the struggle and just say,

"It sounds like you are feeling _____"

and see what happens next. Or try some curiosity,

"Tell me more about that..."

They might be a little surprised because most of us don't listen, instead we think about the next thing we want to say while the other person talks.

These are the things I am seeking to change, it isn't easy, but my hope is that the people I love will remember that about me one day when I leave this earth. My hope is they will say something like this,

"Arlene was a great listener, she really heard me and accepted all of me, the good, the great and the crazy."

It is going to take some work to turn off the dominating advice-giving machine, but I think the people I love are worth it!

Cancer gave my sister a precious gift. She had the chance to experience and receive love from so many people, more than she ever experienced when she was healthy. In fact, just a few years before she was diagnosed, I remember having a conversation with her about how she felt like she had no real friends and she didn't really feel anyone cared about her. Ironically, for her memorial service, we had to rent the community hall because the church and funeral home were too small. There was standing room only... every seat was filled with a person that cared. That tells me we are missing it. We shouldn't have to get a life-threatening disease to feel treasured and loved. There is something wrong with that. Not that we can walk around gushing about how amazing everyone is... or can we? Why not? Isn't it better than complaining about them? We seem to be okay doing that for some reason. So go ahead, tell someone you love why they are so amazing today!! I'm serious, go ahead make their day!

I am so glad that Kathy left this earth knowing she was loved and cared about. I am so thankful that she was surrounded by her dear friends, her children, and her family through the journey. In a way, cancer gave her a gift and she was wise enough to see it. In her last few months, she wrote this when asked "Where is God in all of this?"

He is in the pain...in the tiny moments when there is no pain.
In all the people I meet on this path.
In the doctors and the patients.
In the hearts of my friends, in the hearts of my family,
My children and grand babies as I watch the concern and worry.
In each and every text, email, and phone call.
In every offer to help. The tears and in the joy.
Guiding, carrying, loving, and weeping for He loves me so.
In every hug and every kiss...always watching tenderly.

-Written by Kathy Dawson, 2017

Cancer stole a lot from Kathy, but God used it for good. He used it to show her how treasured, valued and loved she really was. *1 Corinthians 15:55 NIV says* ""Where, O death, is your victory? Where, O death, is your sting?" Death has no victory in Jesus. She left this earth knowing how loved and treasured she is. Verse 54 says *"When the perishable has been clothed with the imperishable, and the mortal with immortality, then the saying that is written will come true: "Death has been swallowed up in victory."* Now she is clothed with immortality and has entered the gates of heaven. Now, in heaven she is constantly in His presence and surrounded by His love. She has no more doubt about who she is and how loved she is. So, death you have NO victory! There is only victory in Jesus.

— *chapter 6* —

LIVE BY FAITH NOT FEAR

PUT FAITH IN the driver's seat of your life, not fear! Is fear holding you back? Is it keeping you from living your best life? For most people the answer is yes. What if you could shake off the shackles of fear and be truly free to live the life of your dreams? It sounds easy but the reality is, it is hard. If every fear we had was completely irrational, we could simply use logic to convince ourselves to have faith. But the truth is some of our fear is legitimate, there is a real risk involved.

I've observed many who let fear drive their life decisions; it is one of the most destructive decisions they make. Fear keeps us small and holds us back from living the life we are truly meant to live. It robs us of our purpose. Most of us are too afraid to take a step outside our comfort zone to pursue what we are really supposed to do. I think if we are honest with ourselves, there is something we know we are supposed to do, but it is buried in fear. We are afraid of the risks; afraid to lose our security; afraid of what others will think of us. Where does all this fear come from? John 10:10 says *"The thief comes* only *to steal* and kill and destroy..." That's right, the enemy wants us to live in fear because it is one of the most effective ways of keeping us from using the talents and gifts that we are meant to share with the world. The talents and gifts that would make this world a better place; bringing a little heaven down here to earth. That's why we have the most fear in the areas of our greatest talents and gifts. It doesn't make sense, does it? In the area we should have the most confidence, we have the most fear. That tells me the enemy is involved. One of the tools that satan uses against us is confusion. He uses it to stop us in our tracks and keep us from doing all the amazing things that God wants us to do in our lives. He uses fear to keep us small and powerless. He uses fear to keep us from our God-given destiny and purpose. He uses it quite effectively too. This is a great motivator for me to overcome my fear. One of my favourite quotes by Joanne Clancy says *"Be the kind of woman who, when your feet hit the floor each morning, the devil says "Oh, no! She's up."* I like to think I aggravate the enemy just a little when I face my fear and do what God is calling me to do.

Fear is the enemy of greatness and the enemy of fulfilment. It keeps you from living a passion-filled, purposeful life. As Myles Munroe *said,*

"The graveyard is the richest place on earth, because it is here that you will find all the hopes and dreams that were never fulfilled, the books that were never written, the songs that were never sung, the inventions that were never shared, the cures that were never discovered, all because someone was too afraid to take that first step."

You were born for a reason, and it is your job to figure out that reason. You were born to make this world a BETTER place. Are you are going through the motions of life to just earn an income? Do you hate your job and dread every minute of it? Then maybe it's time to make a change. Do you daydream about doing something else, but fear is holding you back? Every time you partner with fear instead of faith, the rest of us miss out a little bit. You are robbing us of your talents and gifts. There are people in your life and people you haven't met yet or may never meet that NEED you to do what you are supposed to do! It is important for you and for everyone around you. Every time someone chooses to live their best life it has a *catalyst effect,* and the impact is so great. Every time someone steps out of their comfort zone and into their purpose, using their talents, gifts, and blessings it inspires others to do the same. The definition of catalyst is "an agent that provokes or speeds up significant change or action". We underestimate what happens when we live our dreams and step into our purpose. At times, we minimize its impact by choosing to think it's just all about us. Yes, I believe God truly does want us to be happy and fulfilled but there is even more to it. We underestimate what happens when we live our dreams and step into our purpose. Every time someone chooses FAITH over fear, it gives someone else the courage to do the same. It speeds up change in the world, bringing more goodness into it. You see, YOU have the talents, gifts, and influence that no one else does and the world needs you to use them to make the world a better place. It doesn't end with your little circle of influence though. Your action and faith, will inspire others to take action too! There is a ripple effect. Courage inspires courage. That is the *catalyst effect.* It is impossible to know on this side of heaven the impact that you could have if you stepped into your best life. You have no idea whom you might inspire, empower, and save from a quiet life of desperation. Isn't that inspiring? This is what I think about when I get trapped again by fear. I think of these people, some of them I know and some I do not know and it helps me choose faith once again.

Sometimes our attitudes get distorted. We accept lies as truth. This is a tool of the enemy. We have come to believe that chasing our dreams is selfish. How messed up is that? We think that by putting our dreams first and by using our God-given talents that we are being selfish. I want you to consider something. Maybe ignoring the dreams and talents that you have been given is the most selfish thing you can do? Choosing the safe road has a ripple effect too. It means that people aren't helped, people aren't inspired, the world doesn't improve the way it should. That ripple effect is devastating. The good that should be in the world is stolen with every dream that dies inside of someone.

I have seen a lot of people make excuses about why they can't do what they are meant to do. They try to convince themselves that it is for their children, or their spouse, but the truth is they are scared. Scared to step out. Scared to risk it. I never wanted to use my children or my family responsibilities as an excuse not to do what God called me to do. When I am old, would I tell my grown children that I didn't do it because of them? What kind of example is that? I understand that raising children is a big responsibility and there are sacrifices to be made to do it well. You may have to get creative in how you get started if you have a young family. You may need to start small, but I still believe you can begin on the path towards the life you dream of. There are also different seasons in life where your family may need you more and it is always wise to seek God's wisdom on whether it is the right time to begin something new. If his answer is "Not yet", then I fully support that decision. Perhaps, that just means you should begin to prepare for when the season is right. Farmers prepare in the winter for the spring. They repair their equipment and stock up on what they need for the spring planting so that they are ready when the time comes. We can do the same. Think about what you could do now in preparation for your season of planting. What skills or knowledge could you develop? Could you begin the planning and preparation? Could you ask God to clarify and refine your plans and to connect you with people that could help you achieve it? Pray about your future. Seek the wisdom of God.

Now I know what some of you are thinking because I have had these same thoughts a thousand times. Won't my family suffer if I get serious about my dreams and goals? These thoughts have slowed me down and caused much anguish over the years. I've learned a lot along the way. I've learned to trust myself. I trust that I am tuned into what my family needs and will know when I need to slow down and when it is okay to speed up. Now it might mean that I can't be at every soccer game or every family event, but I am always there when it is important to them. It also might mean I have to change my work plans when it is important to be there for my children. We don't have to go so far as to neglect our families or ignore those we love to live our dreams, but we can stop using them as an excuse. Your child will survive if you miss a few soccer games to do what God has called you to do. In fact, if they see you doing what you are called to do, aren't they more likely to have the courage to do the same? Isn't that what you really want for them? When I look at my children, I see how amazing God made them, I see their uniqueness, their talents and the gifts that God has given them. I know God has amazing plans for their lives and if they choose to live by faith, rather than fear, they will have an amazing, adventure filled, passionate life. If they don't have a role model demonstrating what it means to live by faith, how will they know how to do that? If they learn to stand on the side-lines of life, never truly engaging in what they are meant to do, they'll miss out on the best that God has planned for them. That would be a tragedy. They have so much to offer the world and guess what? So do you!

You are someone's son or daughter and they probably stood beside your crib watching you sleep and wondered how YOU would impact or change the world. Even if your earthly parents didn't do that, your Heavenly Father did! And He still does!

He doesn't wonder what you will do, he is all knowing but He dreams about what He has placed inside you and keeps speaking into it. He is prophesying to you about YOU, and He will continue to speak into what He has placed into you. You just have to start listening and believing in what He is saying.

Read Psalm 139:1-6 and let this sink in:

You have searched me, Lord,
and you know me.
You know when I sit and when I rise;
you perceive my thoughts from afar.
You discern my going out and my lying down;
you are familiar with all my ways.
Before a word is on my tongue
you, Lord, know it completely.
You hem me in behind and before,
and you lay your hand upon me.
Such knowledge is too wonderful for me,
too lofty for me to attain.

God knows your heart. He knows what you secretly desire and dream about. He knows you. He knows what He placed inside you when He created you. He knows the talents and gifts that He needed you to have to do what are meant to do. He has placed people in your life to fan the fire of those passions. He has given you experiences to affirm it and increase your courage but fear has stood in the way. It is time for that to change. I know it is hard to take the first steps, but God is with you. He is behind you and before you and his hands are upon you. You can stand in confidence knowing the Almighty God is with you every step of the way. You, my friend, were fearfully and wonderfully made by a loving God in heaven and you have something beautiful to do in the world. Now, GO DO IT!

When my sister was fighting cancer, there were so many prophetic words given to her about her future and when she passed away it was extremely hard to understand. Why were these words given about her future? Why would God do that if He knew that she would pass away? It was very confusing. But what I have realized is that God will always speak life into us. That is who He is. He is the author and giver of LIFE. His plans for us are good, to give us hope and a future. Even when things aren't going the way He planned for them to go and we are on a vastly different path, like my sister was, He must speak into what He has planned for you. He was speaking those plans into her all her life and I have no doubt that Kathy heard Him.

You see my sister was an incredibly talented, creative woman that was filled with big dreams. I will never forget the last visit I had with her at her farm. We were outside and she had just taught my boys to drive her quad with her oxygen tank in hand. We were leaning on the pickup truck watching them have a blast. She was laughing and cheering them on. This is one of my favourite memories of Kathy. It just captures who she was so perfectly. Then she started telling me how she would like to turn her farm into a retreat centre with horses where people could come to relax and enjoy the peace of nature. She was fighting for every breath and still dreaming big audacious goals. It was who she was, always an idea, always dreaming of creating beautiful places for people to enjoy. To this very day I cannot drive by a Victorian style house without thinking of her dream of having a Bed and Breakfast. It would have been beautiful, welcoming, and peaceful. All her homes were. They were places you didn't want to leave, places you wanted to curl up in and stay forever. Unfortunately, she waited too long to act on many of these dreams. There was always something in the way, some reason not to do it. You see, if you want to accomplish something, you just have to make the decision to accomplish it. There will always be reasons not to and it is easy to see those reasons and give up. Usually, there are also many reasons why you should go for it. If you choose to focus on the reasons why you should do it, it can change your perspective.

For my sister fear got in the way. The voice of fear talked her out of it, over and over. Sometimes it sounded like logic. "I don't have the money" "I don't have time." "It's too difficult." Sound familiar? Like every new entrepreneur has unlimited cash and time! If we allowed those two things to stop us, there would be no new businesses ever! We disguise the self-doubt and fear with these logical reasons. The "realist" comes out to justify why we aren't acting on the burning desire in our hearts. The real reason we don't find a way is we are afraid. Afraid we might fail; afraid we aren't good enough; afraid it will be too much responsibility; afraid we can't handle it. The list is endless, isn't it?

What dream is burning in your heart right now? What dream do you want to breathe life into? God has given you that dream for a reason. It lives in you for a purpose. It isn't silly or unrealistic. It is God-given and important. You are reading this book for a reason, and you are still here living and breathing for a reason. If there is breath in your lungs, then you are here for a reason. Choose today to turn down the volume on the voice of fear and tune into the whisper of faith. It is not too late.

The voice of fear sounds more like it's coming from a megaphone, doesn't it? You know, the one they use when you are in a crowd at a football game to get their message heard. There it is in your head, screaming at you! While the voice of faith is quieter; harder to tune into. It takes quiet reflection and a willingness to listen for it. It is so much easier to let the fear drown it out. Fear is harder to ignore. Fear is a bully, forcing himself into our thoughts. Drowning out the faith and courage. God has a gentler, more subtle way of wooing us into our purpose. That is why we must choose to listen for it, then choose to act. It is also why we must take time to quiet our minds and thoughts and connect with God so we can hear what He is saying to us.

What would happen if we learned to tune into the voice of faith instead? I have found that the more I listen and act on what the voice of faith is saying, the louder it gets and the harder it is to ignore. You start to have this knowing when you get an idea. A certainty that you need to act on it. Mark Twain said, "If you do the things you fear, the death of fear is certain." No, that's not a typo, go back and read that one again, carefully. I'll wait here… Yes, you can slay the dragon of fear in your life simply by doing what you fear. The more often you choose to act in faith instead of fear, the less fear can control you. You can loosen the hold that fear has on you by facing it head on and going for it. Courage is not the absence of fear, it is choosing to act despite the fear. Take some smalls steps to start to build your confidence. Let God show you that you are on the right path. Once you begin to walk in faith and take a few steps, you will also know with more certainty when something is presented that isn't for you to take on. It is easier to let those go because you know what God is calling you into.

So go ahead and decide today to put faith in the driver's seat of your life and see what adventure lies ahead!

– *chapter 7* –

MAKE GOD YOUR PARTNER

I AM CONVINCED that most of us know what we are called to do but very few of us actually ever have the courage to admit it or even say it aloud to ourselves. I believe God has been speaking to each of us throughout our lives and we haven't been listening. We are afraid that we will never accomplish it, and so we tell ourselves,-

"If I never actually recognize what I am supposed to do then I can never fail doing it!"

That thinking is seriously messed up! Think about it – I know I am called to write this book and if I didn't try to write it, never started it, never put pen to paper, I have still been called to do it. Not responding doesn't change that. So now I have guaranteed my failure by ignoring God. All I know is I would rather fail obeying God then fail by ignoring Him. I would rather try and fail then never try at all. I can respond to the call and give it my best shot. In my eyes at least I am giving myself a chance. Kris Vallotton suggests that you ask yourself "What would you be doing if you were ten times braver?" Then he says, if you have any answer whatsoever to this question, your life has been reduced by fear! Wow! I know that is a strong statement.

I have also found that the things I am afraid to speak out loud are often the most important things I am supposed to do.

It's because they mean so much to me, they are so precious! If I say it out loud and someone is not encouraging – raining on my parade – I will be devastated.

Am I alone here? Are there others out there who protect those dreams, hiding them deep within, never acting on them?

It is a little like raising our children. They are so precious to us that we are tempted to hide them away from everything that could possibly harm them. If we did that, we would rob them of the opportunity to grow and become the amazing adults that they are meant to be. They wouldn't be able to function in the real world. If you protect something too much, how can it grow roots and get stronger? Our dreams are like that too. We must open up the door or the window and let a little light shine on them, risking a little rain once in a while in order for them to grow. We muster up the courage and risk it, we uncover those hidden desires. There might be a few rain clouds or even a storm but every once in a while, the sun shines upon them and brings new life to them.

When I became a mom, a more seasoned mom told me that parenting was like having a piece of your heart walking around outside your body. This is so completely true. I must let them go a little – and it is the most vulnerable feeling – but it is part of being a parent. I have felt the same feelings when I've shared my dreams; when I had the courage to voice it out loud to someone. It was vulnerable, and scary; but it was also the first step in making my dreams a reality. As soon as you take that step, your dream will get a little clearer, and a little stronger. It has a little more life! You will begin to visualize it actually happening. Now, something beautiful happens, as you begin to show your dreams to the world, you begin making God your partner in achieving them.

Isn't this amazing? We can make the creator of the universe

our partner! The one who created a universe so large that scholars say it is infinite in size and impossible for man to ever know its size. A universe filled with so many stars, moons, and planets, yet only one perfectly supports human life. It's incredible! And we can partner with Him, to do all we dream and are called to do! As we take those first steps and act in faith, I believe God begins to partner with us. If we are listening to Him, he will guide us, he will show us the best way. He will honour our willingness to walk in faith and be courageous.

Yet, we are filled with doubt.

I understand what it's like to be filled with self-doubt. It plagued me for years until I realized that God, my all-powerful, all-knowing God, was waiting for me to partner with Him and was there to help me out. I realized that by doubting myself, I was doubting that He would give me wisdom, provision, and strength. We talk and sing of His goodness and love but can be completely blind to His desire to help us do what He calls us to do! We rarely take enough action for Him to even have the chance to help us. He can't do it for us. Think about it.

I have been dreaming about this book for a while now, but He can't write it for me, can he? If I put pen to paper, then He can help. He can offer inspiration and ideas through the power of the Holy Spirit, but I have to take the steps.

The Bible is full of stories of people who were called to do something they felt very unqualified and ill-equipped to do. It is such a recurring theme in the Bible. Many of the people who were used in a great way for God felt the most unqualified. So, if you are feeling a little unqualified and wondering why God would ask you to do this, you are in good company. If you aren't a little scared and doubtful, you have probably reduced the vision that God has for your life to something more believable and realistic. It is only when we face our fears, doubts, and insecurities, and choose to trust God's plan for our lives, instead of trusting our own ability, it is only then that we will really soar.

Let's just consider what God called Moses to do. First, he asked Moses to go to Pharoah and talk to him about letting his people out of slavery. What was Moses' response? "Who am I? I am nobody." (See Exodus 3:11) Now, that's self-doubt! What is God's answer amid this doubt? "I will be with you..." He didn't argue with his insecurity, he just says "I will be with you." God fills in all our gaps, makes up for all our weaknesses. It's not about us, it's about who we can be when the King of kings is helping us out!

If God is calling you to do something, you are not doing it alone. Not only are you not alone but you have access to the unlimited resources of your sovereign God. Let this sink in and fill you with Holy confidence and hope. Knowing that you can do all things through Christ who strengthens you. (See Philippians 4:13 NKJV) That verse is my lifeline when I feel insecure about my ability to handle everything God wants me to do. He will be with you and He will give you the strength you need. If you keep reading into Exodus 4, Moses still has doubts and questions about the success of God's plan. To demonstrate his power and convince him, God turns his staff into a snake, turns his hand leprous and then back to normal and tells Moses he will turn water into blood if they still don't believe him. Despite those miraculous demonstrations of power, this is Moses response in verse 10,

> Moses said to the Lord, "Pardon your servant, Lord. I have never been eloquent, neither in the past nor since you have spoken to your servant. I am slow of speech and tongue."

Instead of focusing on what God can do, he looks at his own

weakness. I can only imagine God's frustration! It is so easy to see when reading someone else's story, isn't it? Yet, we do the very same thing so often. I love God's response in verses 11 and 12!

The Lord said to him, "Who gave human beings their mouths? Who makes them deaf or mute? Who gives them sight or makes them blind? Is it not I, the Lord? Now go; I will help you speak and will teach you what to say."

The Lord promises to help him overcome his weakness. I am so glad the Lord is patient with us, aren't you? How easily we forget that He is with us and is empowering us.

I encourage you to breathe life into your dreams by speaking about them. Tell the cheerleaders and supporters in your life (not the negative naysayers who can't wait to rain on your parade). When I started to write this book, I was careful about who I told. My confidence was shaky, at best, in my ability to do this. I needed encouragement from people. I didn't need someone to breathe life into my doubts, I was doing a pretty good job of that myself. Seek out someone in your life that takes risks and has done something courageous themselves, they are more likely to encourage you than someone that has played it safe most of their life. I know they are hard to find, aren't they? Most of us don't have a lot of examples of people stepping out and doing what they really want to do. They are out there and if you start looking you will find a few. After years of chasing my dreams, I have learned who is safe to entrust my dreams to and who will do their best to suffocate them. In the movie, Pursuit of Happyness, the main character (played by Will Smith) tells his son this "If you have a dream, you have to protect it." Be discerning and wise about who you entrust your precious dream to. You are careful about who to leave your precious children with when you go out, aren't you? You choose someone caring, trustworthy and responsible not just someone who is available.

I often feel a prompting from God to share what I am doing with people. That is when I know I must share it. I have realized that He wants me to share it for a few reasons and it is not just for my own encouragement. Many of the people I have felt prompted to tell have been great encouragers and that has helped me act. Some of them have been able to give me some direction on how to complete this book. They have connections or resources that could help me through the process. Others are on a similar journey and they need encouragement. This is what I have found so amazing! Several of my friends had started writing or had been writing for a while. We have connected more closely than before because of that. It also gave me more courage to know that I wasn't the only crazy one that thought she could write a book! I also met more people that were involved in writing or publishing than ever before in the months after I made the decision to write this book. Now you might be tempted to think of those encounters as "coincidences" but I know it was God's way of reminding me of my decision and affirming that it was what He wanted me to do. Julia Cameron in her book The Artist's Way explains it this way,

> *"The reason we think it's weird to imagine an unseen helping hand is that we still doubt that it's okay for us to be creative. With this attitude firmly entrenched, we not only look all gift horses in the mouth but also swat them on the rump to get them out of our lives as fast as possible."*

What does it mean to look a gift horse in the mouth? Merriam-Webster says it means to look at the gift in a critical way. There are no coincidences, they are gifts from God. Let's stop swatting away God's encouragement by labelling them as such! If you are feeling uncertain, He wants to give you certainty. If you feel prompted to mention it in a conversation, go for it. Some of the most random people have given me the most encouragement. It reaffirms the call that God has placed on me. It encourages me to take the next step. It has helped me shut out those doubtful voices that come from within.

When we take that first act of courage and put ourselves out there, God meets us there and begins the process of affirming and guiding our steps. God is using those people. Just as God used Aaron to increase Moses' confidence. Despite God's encouragement and demonstration of power, Moses still had doubt about his own ability and begs God to send someone else. God realizes he is not going to overcome this doubt on his own and sends his brother Aaron to go with him. Aaron is strong where Moses is weak. He is eloquent and well spoken. This gives Moses the confidence to do what God has asked. Isn't it comforting that God didn't give up on Moses and go find another more willing person? God didn't need Aaron to go with Moses to accomplish his goal, but Moses did. God realized this and provided Aaron to support him on his quest. God will provide the support we need to if we partner with him.

God is so good. When the voices of doubt got louder and started to drown out the confidence, when hope started to fade, I would get an email or text from someone that inspired or encouraged me to believe in my dream and keep going. God is paying attention and providing all that I need to do this. Like an attentive gardener, he sees the weeds that threaten to choke out what He has planted and purposed for my life, and he carefully pulls them out. He provides the sunshine that is needed to keep them growing through those encouraging people. Slowly the dream takes shape and has a little more clarity. It can only happen if you take the seed that He gave you and place it in fertile ground. Take it out of its protected safe place and put it outside, expose it to the light. Of course, you wonder,

"Will the wind will blow it away?"

"Will a bird snatch it up?"

If you take the risk and expose your dream to the elements, trust that your God will show up and partner with you. I truly believe that God will provide the encouragement, if only you will take that first step.

So, who are your cheerleaders? Who can you count on for support through your journey? Write those names down right now and make a plan to talk to them about your dream.

1. _____

2. _____

3. _____

4. _____

Now commit to having some vulnerable conversations; telling each of them your dream and the action you are taking towards it. Take them for coffee or lunch. It is important that you take this step because when you step out and give your dream a voice, it automatically gives others permission to do the same. That prompting that you are feeling to tell someone may not be just for your encouragement. God may want to use you to encourage them. Maybe there is a dream burning in their heart and they don't have the courage to take the first step. When you share your heart, it gives them permission to speak about what they really want and bring it to life with their words.

It is also important to know who you need to protect your dream from. Come on, you know who I am talking about! I know we don't like to admit that some of the people we love and care about aren't very encouraging. It is difficult to put that into words, but I want to encourage you to do that, too. Who will rain on your parade? Who will tell you that you are crazy and encourage you to stick with the small plans for your life?

1._____

2._____

3._____

You need to know who to avoid when you are taking those first steps and your confidence is low. It doesn't mean you keep it from them forever. Just like you need to protect a small plant from the wind and the hail; you need to protect your dream in the early stages. It is just too easy to get discouraged. Your roots aren't deep enough to withstand the storm. Give your roots some time to go deep before you expose it to the naysayers.

I know for sure if you take these first steps that God will meet you there and provide the encouragement you need. He is a good God and knows what you need to move forward. I am so thankful that He is a patient and loving God. He will partner with you. Just as he partnered with Moses to free the Israelites. If you continue to read the story of how the Lord used Moses to free his people, you will see how He partnered with him. The Lord provided the way. Moses kept seeking the Lord and the Lord gave him the instructions. Moses was obedient and followed the instructions God gave him and fulfilled his destiny. Now you will notice, he guides him step by step. He doesn't outline all the steps at the beginning. He requires us to have faith to take those first steps without knowing the whole plan.

> *For in it the righteousness of God is revealed from faith to faith; as it is written, "The just shall live by faith."* Romans 1:17 NKJV

We see another example when Saul (Paul) was persecuting Jesus. Saul was threatening the followers of Jesus and planning to bring them bound to Jerusalem to be punished. God needed to get his attention to stop the persecution. Let's read Acts 9:3-7

> *As he journeyed, he came near Damascus, and suddenly a light shone around him from heaven. Then he fell to the ground, and heard a voice saying to him, "Saul, Saul, why are you persecuting Me?" And he said, "Who are You, Lord?" Then the Lord said, "I am Jesus, whom you are persecuting. It is hard for you to kick against the goads." So he, trembling and astonished, said, "Lord, what do You want me to do?" Then the Lord said to him, "Arise and go into the city, and you will be told what you must do."* NKJV

Saul reacts with immediate obedience asking "What do you want me to do?" God revealed who Jesus was to him and his response was obedience. Without this attitude, he could not have done all that he did for the kingdom. This explains why God chose Saul, he knew he was an obedient follower. God just gives him one step; he is told to go into the city and then he will be told what to do. Saul had to act in faith without knowing the full plan. If we know the whole plan upfront, then a lot of faith isn't really needed. God wants us to move in faith. From faith to faith. Listening to him and obeying. This builds trust and relationship between you and the Almighty God. Knowing that all he has planned for you is good. A partnership between you and God.

Now let's go back to Moses, God gives him clear instructions to get started and warns him that Pharaoh will not agree easily. God prepared Moses as he went. He also encouraged him with some promises. He promised to bring them to a "land flowing with milk and honey" (see Exodus 3:8) Isn't that a great promise? A land flowing with abundance. It didn't just have a little milk and honey; it was flowing with it. Now the journey to this land of abundance was not easy but it was so worth it. He also promises in Exodus 3:21-22 that the Egyptians will fund their trip to freedom! What a great God! The Egyptians had enslaved and oppressed them for a long time. Not only will he provide the way to freedom but those who oppressed and mistreated them will end up funding the way! What great retribution for all the years they enslaved God's people. This is the same God we partner with when we answer the call on our life! The God of Abraham, Isaac, and Jacob. You too can partner with Him when you go from faith to faith and take the first step.

– chapter 8 –

WRITE IT DOWN

NOW THAT YOU have made it all seem more real by telling a few people what you are going to do, what's next? WRITE IT DOWN!

> *"...write the vision, and make it plain on tablets..."* Habakkuk 2:2 KJV

Why does He tell us to do that? I believe there are many reasons.

First, writing it down forces you to clarify what the vision actually is. The more clarity you have the easier it is to take action. When the idea for this book first came to me, I wasn't sure if it was meant to be written for a secular audience or for believers. As I clarified the vision for the book, I realized that this is a message for His people! God wants to use this book to empower his people to walk in faith and do all He has called them to do so we can change the world around us. Writing down my ideas for the book helped me see that. "Write it down and make it plain" are God's instructions. Writing it down makes it clear and refines your vision for it.

Writing it down also gives it permanence. It goes from being a fleeting thought to something more concrete. It's a permanent record of what you are dreaming of that declares, "This is what I am called to do and I am doing it!" In the early 1900s, Napoleon Hill was hired by Andrew Carnegie to study the most successful people in the world and one of the common factors he found in his study is that they write down their goals. This isn't something new. It isn't something the new personal growth industry made up. It was written in the Bible, and we continue to see evidence of it working today.

Writing it down also calls you into action. The next line in Habakkuk 2:2 is, "That he may run who reads it." Don't you just love how God hints at things in the word? He doesn't always state things in the most obvious way. It is like he wants us to dig for it, to ponder, to ask what does this mean? He wants us to seek after it. Jeremiah 29:13 says "You will seek me and find me when you seek me with all your heart." It's like a treasure hunt. So let's dig in and see what we can find!

First, we are instructed to write it down. Then ask yourself "What is the purpose of writing it down?" It might seem obvious, but I am thinking to read it! So, what happens when we read it? Our desire to run with it increases. I have been setting goals for nearly two decades since I started my own business. I was taught to write goals down in the present tense. For example "I am writing a book this year" instead of "I am going to write a book". See the difference? One calls you into immediate action and one puts the action out there sometime in the future. The future tense tells our brain that we are doing that later, somewhere down the road, not now. When we use the present tense, it tells our brain we are taking action now! The word says "That he may RUN..." It doesn't say "write it down so that sometime later in the future someone else will run". The word indicates that the running will start now. If we write down our goals and we read them, our desire to act on them NOW increases. It keeps them fresh in our mind. Our lives are full of distractions, so this is crucial. We need to keep what's most important in the forefront. By reading our goals daily it reminds us to focus on what is really important. The focus on the goal is what keeps us from getting distracted. There are so many options out there. If we aren't clear about what we want and what God wants in our life, it is very easy to get pulled away. It is easy to put our time, effort, and resources into something else. Something that is less important or isn't ours to do. There are many good things to pursue, and we must be sure that we are pursuing the goals that we are meant to complete. Otherwise, we may get distracted and chase after something totally different and miss what God wants for us.

The NIV version of this verse says it a little differently and I think it is worth pondering. It says, *Then the LORD replied: "Write down the revelation and make it plain on tablets so that a herald may run with it."*

We don't use the word herald anymore so I took a minute to look it up. One of the definitions in the Oxford Learners Dictionary is "something that shows that something else is going to happen soon." I love that! Can't you feel the excitement of expectation in that definition? Writing it down is like the announcement that something better is going to happen in your life. I imagine God and his angels up in heaven running through the streets of gold announcing that something wonderful is going to happen in your life!

Setting financial goals has been a great teacher of this principle for me. Years ago, my husband and I set a goal to pay off some debt. We wrote it down and we started to track it. Then the temptation came, the temptation to spend instead of paying down our debt. It would have been way more fun in the moment to spend it instead of paying the debt down. We were tempted over and over. Getting clarity as a couple on our goal and writing it down, held us accountable to each other and to our goal. That made it easier to say no to those things that tempted us. We had a vision for what we wanted – To be debt free! The vision reduced the pain of saying no to lesser things. The vision kept us focused on it. We made a lot of progress on paying down our debt that year. I'm not exactly sure if we paid it all down and reached the goal 100% but we made so much progress and it taught us the value of setting goals together and using the goal to help us make decisions. The question we kept asking ourselves as we made financial decisions that year was, "Is this aligned with our goal of paying off our debt?" If the answer was no, then the decision was easy. It was also more empowering than saying "We can't afford this" or "We are too broke to do this…" Instead of focusing on being broke, we were focused on the vision of having no debt. When asked to spend on something that was not in our budget, we said "That is not aligned with our goals right now" instead of saying "We are too broke right now." Can you see the difference? One is discouraging and one empowers you to stick with your goal and reach it! We had a vision of paying off that life-limiting debt and that vision guided our decisions.

So we write it down, then we read it and run with it. What's next? Habakkuk 2:3 says:

> *"The vision is yet for an appointed time; but at the end it will speak and it will not lie. Though it tarries wait for it; because it will surely come; it will not tarry."*

God may place a desire in our hearts or give us a dream well in advance of it actually happening. Most of us aren't patient enough to keep focused on it until it happens. We live in a microwave society, a high-tech society and it is causing us to be less patient. We have come to expect everything in 30 seconds or less. If there is a delay, it really messes us up! Guess what? (I know you don't want to hear this but) there will be delays!

What happens when we are setting goals, working hard for them, and they don't come quite as quickly as we expect? I have seen a lot of people give up. I have actually heard them say "Well if it is this difficult, I guess it isn't God's will for my life." What?! I think we need to go back to our bible and refresh our memories. God is much less worried about time than we are! I guess that happens when you are the God of eternity.

Let's read Daniel 10:12-14;

Then he said, "Don't be afraid, Daniel. Since the first day you began to pray for understanding and to humble yourself before your God, your request has been heard in heaven. I have come in answer to your prayer. But for twenty-one days the spirit prince of the kingdom of Persia blocked my way. Then Michael, one of the archangels, came to help me, and I left him there with the spirit prince of the kingdom of Persia. Now I am here to explain what will happen to your people in the future, for this vision concerns a time yet to come."

It is interesting that he starts with "Don't be afraid, Daniel." When there is a delay, fear will set in. We start to fear that it won't happen or maybe it isn't God's will or maybe I am not good enough. We must shut down the fear in those moments and remember God's word. Then God reassures Daniel that his prayers had been heard. God hears your prayers too. Sometimes I pray over and over like he hasn't heard them the first time. God gives us that reassurance that he has heard you. Verse 13 describes the spiritual warfare that the angel faced while coming to help. This is a good reminder to us as believers. When we step into our God ordained purpose, the enemy will try to stop us. He will try to abort the plans of God in your life. We must stand strong and writing our goals down helps us do that. Lastly, he says that "this vision concerns a time yet to come". Your vision also concerns a time yet to come. This reminds us of God's perfect timing not ours. He knows the perfect time for it. He knows exactly how and when it needs to come together for it to do all that he has planned it to do. Let's pause here and thank God for HIS timing. It is always perfect.

We tend to think very short term but God sees the whole picture. He sees how everything fits together in his perfect timing. Just think about Abraham. God promises him a son in his old age. Not only was he old but so was his wife, well past childbearing years. Abraham is so faithful that he believes God despite the biological difficulties but then he has to wait. That is where we falter isn't it? The waiting... it is so hard to wait for what we desire.

Abraham and Sarah falter. Sarah, focused on the limitations of her old earthly body, hatches a plan to help out God, and Abraham agrees to go along with the idea. She gave Hagar, her Egyptian slave to Abraham, to be his wife, and he slept with her. That wasn't God's plan, but they couldn't wait. It is easy to judge Sarah's impatience, but we do this all the time. Running ahead of God, hatching our own plan, instead of waiting on the Lord. Perhaps, that even delayed the birth of Isaac longer than God intended. Now we can't really judge them for faltering in the waiting, can we? If I was 80 and God promised me a child, I would likely expect it to happen fairly soon. I am sure getting even older before having a child seemed crazy to Abraham and Sarah; after all those years they finally received the promise they had prayed for, and they were expecting an immediate result. But God says "The vision is yet for an appointed time..." God has a perfect time planned for your dream to happen. We have to trust Him in that. If we know we are doing what He wants us to do, then we can rest in that and trust His timing. "At the end it will speak, it will not lie.". We can trust God in the waiting, trust His perfect timing.

When my children were little God gave me a vision about my business. I knew that it was supposed to be growing, thriving, and be an inspiration to others but it wasn't. We were stuck, it wasn't growing, we had plateaued and nothing I did seemed to change that. It was incredibly frustrating, but I realize now the vision was yet for an appointed time. What I visualized happening is actually what is happening right now! 5-6 years later. Looking back, I am thankful for God's perfect timing. He knew the real desire of my heart was to be with my young children. If my business had exploded at that time, I would have felt so torn between my boys and my business. Instead, he used that time to prepare me for this time, for the harvest. "Though it tarries, wait for it."

The word "tarry" isn't really used anymore so, what does it mean? It means to be delayed in leaving a place. I believe this word is used for a reason. It isn't just delayed or held up but it is delayed in leaving a place. I see this visualization in that word- like your dream or vision is placed in God's hands. Sometimes it feels like it is stuck, and it is frustrating but it is actually just being held in God's hand for the appointed time. To us it feels like it is late or being delayed, so He uses that word "tarry". He wants us to trust His timing. We aren't always ready for it as quickly as we think we are. So He holds it in his hands; cherishing it; protecting it, until the appointed time. If we allow him to prepare us in the waiting, we will be ready for it and the blessing will be that much better!

Perhaps in the waiting our prayer should be "Prepare me Lord!" Use the waiting to prepare yourself. What do you need to work on to be better prepared to achieve this goal? There may be a skill that you need to acquire and there are classes you could take to acquire that skill. Perhaps there is some area in your personal growth that you need to improve? If you use the waiting period to grow and strengthen yourself, you will be better prepared for what is ahead. I chose to hire a business coach during my waiting period. With his help I worked on the areas of leadership that caused me stress and self-doubt. This prepared me to lead a larger more successful organization. It was so valuable. I am thankful for the waiting now. I realize I needed it to be ready for the growth that is happening now.

Let's look at the next line in Habakkuk *"Because it will surely come; it will not tarry."* God reassures us that it will surely come. I love how the word is written. He just said "though it tarries" and now He is saying "it will not tarry". Don't you just want to say "Which is it Lord? It is tarrying or not?" I believe it is written this way so that we must wrestle with it to find the meaning. God doesn't spoon feed us like a baby. He wants us to chew on it, digest it, ponder it. That's why you could read the Bible over and over and keep getting new revelation. I believe he is just saying that it will feel like it is *not* coming. It will feel like it is being held up. You will feel impatient and frustrated BUT wait for it. Don't give up. Don't stop believing. Don't lose faith in what God has planned for you.

In our microwave-smart-device-high speed-internet world we have lost the ability to WAIT. We want everything NOW or even 30 seconds ago. We don't like delays. Did you know that one of the greatest indicators of whether a child will be successful in life is their ability to delay gratification? In the 1960's Walter Mischel studied 4 and 5-year-olds, and the impact that delaying gratification had on their success in life, in his famous Marshmallow experiment. He gave the 4 and 5 year-olds one marshmallow and told them that if they could wait 15 minutes before eating it then he would give them a second marshmallow. Then he left the single marshmallow on the table and left the room for 15 minutes. Some of the children ate the marshmallow right away. Some of them struggled and tried to resist eating it but after a few minutes gave in and ate it. Some of them waited the whole 15 minutes and received the second marshmallow. Years later they followed up with these children and remarkably they found that the ones that waited were more successful in many areas of life.

After years of training people that are transitioning from being employees to entrepreneurs, I have observed the same thing. The ones that are impatient and expect their actions to yield immediate results, don't succeed. They were accustomed to putting in 40 hours and getting their paycheque that Friday. That isn't how it works as an entrepreneur. Sometimes you put in 40 hours and there is no paycheque. If, however, you keep going and keep doing what you need to do to grow your business, it starts to pay off, and you end up with bigger paycheques than you would have ever had as an employee. The fortune is in handling the delay. It isn't that these people wouldn't have succeeded if they had stuck it out. Many of them were more talented and skilled than the people that are succeeding now but they couldn't handle the delays. They gave up too soon. They couldn't manage the disappointment; the failure; the waiting.

The ability to wait for something better has a big impact. God knew this so He tells us to wait. Even when it feels like it isn't happening, wait for it. His promise is that it will NOT TARRY. If we are faithful in our actions and in our belief, it will surely come, it will not tarry.

Between the Writing and the Running

What is happening between the writing and the running? I believe that God is working. If he is your partner, then he is working with you. If we are obedient and write it, God will give you instructions on the running. One mistake we make is thinking we have to have all the ideas, strategies, and steps when we have a dream. This makes us hesitant and doubtful in the beginning because we may only have a basic idea. We may even feel a little silly writing it down because it seems vague and unclear. If you know He is calling you and He has placed this desire in your heart, then you have that 'knowing' that this is something that He wants you to do. Just write it down, no matter how unclear or vague it may seem to you. Then watch him clarify it for you! That act of obedience will activate the clarification process.

You see you can always rewrite it as He clarifies and refines your vision. It's not a one-time thing. Now in the Bible era rewriting was a little harder. They were, at times, writing on stone tablets and I am sure paper was difficult to acquire. Our tablets today are so easy to edit. You do not need to draw up a perfect first draft. One of the pieces of advice that I received when I started to write was that it was okay to write a mediocre first draft. You have to start somewhere. Accept that it isn't going to be perfect the first time and embrace its imperfection. It is that simple act of faith that activates God in the spirit realm and - if we stay connected to Him; in His presence - the clarity will come. He will show you the first step. He will provide the inspiration, the confirmation, and the desire.

Write it down, that perfectly imperfect vision that He is developing inside you. It's like growing a baby in your womb. At first it doesn't look like a baby at all. Remember that first ultrasound? They show you this blob on the screen and say it is your baby. It barely resembles anything human, but we have faith that it will develop into a perfect, beautiful baby. Trust that God will help you develop your dream into something beautiful too. Write it down and then start praying like crazy for that first step. Pray for ideas, strategies, and wisdom. Pray that He would direct your steps.

Pray the word of God over your dreams:

The LORD directs the steps of the godly. He delights in every detail of their lives. Psalm 37:23 NLT

Seek his will in all you do, and he will show you which path to take. Proverbs 3:6 NLT

Ask yourself this question- What would I do if there were no obstacles? You know, no barriers of time or money or geography or resources. What would you do then? If it's anything other than what you are doing right now, then you have let fear reduce your life. You have let fear stop you. Let that sink in, I'll wait here. Now, have the courage to WRITE DOWN the answer. What would I do IF I DIDN"T CONSIDER THE OBSTACLES?

_____

_____

_____

_____

I am serious. Write it down. Those lines on this page should not be blank. There is an answer burning in your heart. He came so you could have life and live it abundantly. He didn't come so you could go through the motions, living a quiet life of desperation. Be courageous and write it down! Go for it! So what is the next step? Now that you have allowed yourself to breathe a little life into your dream, ask yourself "What could the next step be?" If you are not sure and have no ideas, start praying for ideas. Ask God to reveal it. Then wait in expectation of His answer, though it tarries, it will come. God loves our expectation. He loves it when we pray expecting something to happen. In Acts 4, the man at the Gate called Beautiful asked Peter and John for money and then looked up at them expecting an answer. His expectation was met with way more than he was asking for! Look up, expecting an answer. Seek out an answer. The definition of seek is to look for, attempt to obtain or ask for something. There is action implied in the word. It is a verb. Once you have asked for the next step, start looking for the answer. It isn't a passive thing. We don't ask and then hope that maybe God will hijack the billboard on your route to the office and tell you exactly what to do. It isn't that obvious usually. You have to go looking. There is that beautiful word again "GO!" get out there looking for the answer.

Now it is possible that you know the next step, isn't it? You may already know the next step or even two, so get started! This is where the running starts! Run with what you have, trusting Him to provide the rest of the steps along the way. Run and allow him to reveal it from 'faith to faith' as it says in Romans 1:17. Otherwise, we wouldn't need faith, would we? He gives us the first step or two, and we have to ACT in faith to receive the next few steps. Think about Abraham, God tells him to leave his family and his home and "Go to the land I will show you."

The really incredible part of the story is that Abraham went! He left his home, his land, and his people to go somewhere? What beautiful, incredible faith. The Lord didn't tell him where, He just told him to go.

> *It was by faith that Abraham obeyed when God called him to leave home and go to another land that God would give him as his inheritance. He went without knowing where he was going. And even when he reached the land God promised him, he lived there by faith—for he was like a foreigner, living in tents. And so did Isaac and Jacob, who inherited the same promise. Abraham was confidently looking forward to a city with eternal foundations, a city designed and built by God.*
> Hebrews 11:8-10 NLT

Abraham had to trust God to direct his steps and take him where he was supposed to go. Abraham trusted that His plan was good, better than what he had already. If Abraham didn't trust God, he never would have gone. This type of trust and obedience is so rare. If we can't see the outcome or destination, we don't go. We play it safe, settling for way less than God's best for our lives. We forget the promise at the end of what God said, "I will show you." God promised Abraham that He would show him the way. He would show him where he was to go. All Abraham had to do was to trust the promise and do what God asked him to do.

I believe this is happening all the time with God's people. He is telling them "Go to the land I will show you" and we aren't listening. We don't trust Him enough to go. It may look different than it did for Abraham. It may not be a physical journey away from our home or our family. He may be telling you to make a career change, start a business, paint the painting, or sing the song. That simple act could be the act that opens a new door in your life. A door that leads to life abundantly! Responding to Him could be the catalyst that takes you into the land He has planned for you. It takes faith, doesn't it? We want it all laid out, clear as day, steps A to Z. We want certainty. We want God to lay it all out in front of us so we can decide, before we go, if we want to go. That's not how it works with God. If I had known in advance exactly how the journey of building a business was going to be, I am not sure I would have done it. The ups, downs, detours, and setbacks. The person I was at the beginning of the journey was not ready for all that. The journey is what prepares and strengthens us. It is also where the greatest blessings are found. Will you have total certainty and a perfectly laid out plan? It's not likely. Partnering with God has way more adventure than that!! There is no certainty, only faith. If it were so certain, we wouldn't need faith. We need to surrender that certainty and place our lives in His hands, trusting Him to lead us.

Sounds a little scary, doesn't it? I agree, but what if it were the safest place that you could be? In His will is the safest place for you. It may be a wild ride, but God is your seatbelt and your airbag. If the essence of God is His goodness, then you know His plans for your life can only be good. It won't always be easy, but the results will be good. We need to pray about this so we can embrace the unknown and start the journey.

Pray this with me:

"Lord Jesus, I surrender the certainty that I crave, and I give it all to you. I lay the plans for my life down in total surrender. You know the plans you have for me, plans to prosper me not to harm me. I lay down my need for worldly certainty at the foot of the cross and ask you for the courage and strength to go to the land you will show me."

Our only certainty in this world is in Him. Knowing who He is and knowing His goodness. That is all the certainty we need.

For I know the plans I have for you," says the LORD. "They are plans for good and not for disaster, to give you a future and a hope. Jeremiah 29:11 (NLT)

– chapter 9 –

DON'T WAIT TO DO WHAT YOU LOVE

A FEW YEARS ago, my life coach asked me a question that I really struggled to answer. "What do you do for fun?" "Fun?" was my response. Like this was some foreign concept or a word I didn't understand. It was like I was wondering "What does fun have to do with winning in life and getting my business to the next level?" After all, that was the reason I was paying him (paying him very well I might add) and he is asking me about fun?! Of course, he didn't let me off the hook. He made me answer the question. After an awkward silence, I came up with a few things, but it was incredibly difficult and uncomfortable.

At the time I wasn't having much fun at all. Fun was something I would do later, after I was successful and had achieved my goals. I was too busy raising my children and building my business. It was so bad that when my son was in preschool the teachers did a Mother's Day craft and had the children answer some questions about their moms and the teacher wrote the answers on the craft. One of the questions was "What does Mom do for fun?" His answer was "Work." Now I tried to spin my reaction to his answer and say that he thought I was having fun at work because I love what I do so much but in reality, that probably isn't the truth. He probably couldn't think of anything else that I did outside of housework and office work. Sad, isn't it? I have learned since then that putting off all fun until you reach some magical moment when you will suddenly have time does not work well. Weaving fun into your life NOW while you are chasing your dreams and goals is essential fuel for you to get there. Taking time to just have fun reenergizes you and you need a lot of energy to reach your goals. Having fun with the people you love also builds stronger bonds and relationships. Taking time away to just have fun reduces stress. Our brains actually produce more serotonin when we play. Serotonin is a powerful neurotransmitter that helps our bodies in many different ways. It has been named "the feel-good hormone". Serotonin gives us that relaxed, confident and happy feeling. Lack of serotonin has been linked to increased anxiety, depression and even heart disease. Serotonin helps you feel happier, sleep better, and helps you clear your thinking and increases brain function. Fun is something our body really needs to function properly.

As a goal-oriented person, trying hard to build my business and have a better life, I had embraced the idea that fun was a waste of time and if I wasn't producing some tangible result then I was wasting time. The essence of fun is that we do it just for the joy of doing it. Science has proven that having fun isn't a waste of time at all. It helps us to become stronger, more resilient, more productive people. This seems counter-productive, doesn't it? I completely understand that thinking. I was that Type A focused person; in fact, it is still a struggle for me to check out and just have fun. That was my reaction when my coach told me I should have more fun. I was already stressed for time and struggling to do everything I was expected to do. What I discovered when I started to have more fun is that I had more energy for my children and business. I could think more clearly at work and got more done in less time and most importantly, I started to enjoy my work again.

Ask yourself this question, what brings you pure joy, energy, or makes you laugh or makes you smile?

If you can't think of anything, alarm bells should be going off right now! Perhaps you have neglected yourself so much you don't even know what you like to do. We are so busy making sure our children, our spouses, or our bosses have their needs met that what we enjoy gets lost and forgotten. That was what had happened to me before my coach asked me that question. I was pouring all my energy into my children and my business, and the result was I felt stressed and empty even though I loved my work and my children. I want to help you rediscover your fun factor. Ask yourself these questions,

1. What did I do as a child for fun?
   - Did you get lost in crafts or puzzles or Lego?
   - Was it a sport or music?
   - Singing, painting, art or nature?
   - Maybe you remember spending hours playing with a pet and it was pure joy.

2. What do you or did you lose track of time doing?
   - When are those moments when you are so fully present and filled with so much satisfaction?
   - What can you lose yourself in?
   - What is so enjoyable that you totally lose track of time?

Perhaps just thinking about it right now brings peace and joy to your soul. One of those things for me is horseback riding.

I had wanted a horse since I was about 12 years old. I had never owned one but had friends when I was a preteen who had horses and even before I spent any time with horses, I was drawn to them. Since my sister passed away, I decided it was time to make that dream come true. My sister had bought her horse a few years before she got sick and loved to ride. It inspired me that she had acted on that dream in her late 40s. So, I decided to buy my sister's horse, Gus, the summer after she passed away. The decision didn't make a lot of logical sense at the time – we didn't have a place to keep him, we lived in the city – but I just knew I had to do this. It was one of those God moments, when everything came together so perfectly and easily, I just knew it was meant to be. It was a Friday morning. I was praying. I wasn't praying for anything specifically, just talking to God like you would a best friend. My mind drifted, and I started to tell God about how much I missed Kathy. That led to thoughts about her horse and how nice it would be to buy him. I had this sudden urgency to make it happen, right now. First, I sent my brother-in-law a text and asked if he would sell him to me. He agreed. Second, I found an ad for horse boarding, and arranged to go see it. Then I called a friend and asked if we could borrow his horse trailer and truck to pick him up. Within hours I had it all worked out. Within weeks he was at the farm near our house. Over the summer, we spent lots of time out at the farm where he was staying. One thing I learned after a few visits is that time would fly when we were out there. I would totally lose track of time. It would feel like we had been there 2 hours and it was closer to 4 or 5 hours. It was pure joy! There is nothing like the feeling of losing track of time doing something you love. Getting a horse has taught me more about being present in the moment than I ever imagined. Somehow the horses know if you aren't present, and it doesn't go well. It is such a joy to totally immerse yourself in the moment doing something you love.

It makes me wonder if most of us are missing that in our lives. Could it be that this is making us overly stressed and causing all sorts of mental illness? Our lives are so busy; we struggle to put our phones down during family dinners and date nights. We are rarely present; in the moment; forgetting everything else. When I was out with my boys and the horses, I was forced to be completely present. I would leave the phone in the truck, and I didn't own a watch, so I would totally lose track of time. It was incredible how the time would fly by. My husband would laugh when I was leaving to see the horses and I would tell him I should be home at a certain time. He knew it would be 1-2 hours later than what I had planned every time! Even if I carry my phone, it is difficult to even check it. You must pay attention to the horse when you are working with them, or they end up doing something silly. It has been an incredible gift to be able to turn off everything else and just focus solely on the horse, the beautiful scenery, and enjoying the moment.

What is burning in your heart right now?

Something you love to do and wish you could do more of. Maybe you are coming up with a laundry list of reasons of why that it is unrealistic and not possible right now. If your primary objection is time. I challenge you not to allow yourself to use time as an excuse. Life is way too short. If you can't find a few hours to do something you really love and enjoy then something might need to change. When I bought my horse, I was running my business, was the primary caregiver for our 2 children, and working on some home repairs so we could list our home for sale. I had no extra time. I was a little naive about the time I would need to invest into a horse, as well, and I am thankful for that. I probably wouldn't have done it, had I known how much time it takes. The funny thing is that I found the time. So, take time out of the equation and just let yourself acknowledge something that is important to you.

If finances are the main reason that you aren't doing more of what you love then let's think outside the box for a minute. I don't want you to overspend and put yourself in a difficult position. That goes against everything I believe in. That would not be wise. I believe there is probably a cost-effective way or even a free way to do it and you just haven't figured that out yet. For example, if you love horses and my story resonates with you but you can't afford to buy a horse and then pay for its upkeep and boarding then doing what I did would be a very bad idea. I'll let you in on a little secret though, there are horse owners EVERYWHERE with horses that don't get ridden often enough. They would love to have someone come and spend time with their horses. Start talking about your love of horses and you will find someone with a horse that needs some love and attention guaranteed!

Start thinking of other ways to do more of what you love. Think outside the box. If you love animals, but you can't have a pet for some reason, you could volunteer at an animal shelter. If you would love to take an art class or writing class but can't afford it, look online for lessons on those topics or find a more informal option like a Meetup group that meets regularly to encourage each other or offers free instruction. It is amazing what you can find for free! If you love to sing, find a choir or group you can join for free. If you love a sport, find a community team you can join for a low cost. Most of the time there is low-cost way or free way to get started. Start there and who knows where it will take you.

You deserve the opportunity to do something you really enjoy. It will feed your spirit and fill you in a way that you can't imagine. You will have more to give as a result. For a long time, I lived in fear of spending time doing something I really loved, because I thought it was selfish. With a business to run I was already spending time away from my family to work. It seemed selfish to leave them for other reasons, too. What I realized is that I can pursue some of the things I enjoy, because it fills me up. It gives me more energy. I have more to give them when I return. I feel 10 years younger since I bought our horse. I am more energized than ever. I challenge you to give up the fear that it is going to take away from your life and relationships. That is all it is, an irrational fear. Trust yourself. Trust that you will know how to keep it in balance, so it doesn't take away from your family. We fear so many things that will never even happen. Look for fun things you can do with your spouse and children. My children loved the horse, too. We had great times together, out with the horses - away from TV and technology - in the fresh air. It has added so much to our lives. I also like to think I am setting a good example for them. Living my life on purpose is showing them how to live a full, vibrant life. Living the type of life that I wish for them to live.

Happiness is a Great Decision

Life is too short to live unhappy, and unfulfilled. Being unhappy has so many negative side effects on our bodies, there is no way that God wants us to live that way.

For I know the plans I have for you," declares the LORD, "plans to prosper you and not to harm you, plans to give you hope and a future. Jeremiah 29:11 NIV

Notice He doesn't say His plans involve endless suffering and desperation. There will be trials along the way but if there are only trials perhaps it is time to consider a new direction.

Your happiness is ultimately your responsibility. It's no one else's job to make you happy. No one else can do it for you. In fact, when we make it someone else's responsibility, we are more likely to end up unhappy. Think about it this way, I have found it quite difficult to figure out what makes me happy, I have invested years into personal growth, taken courses to heal my emotional wounds, and hired life coaches. Is it fair to even expect my spouse or my children to figure it out? We are complex human beings and it's difficult to figure out what we are meant to do and what we really want and enjoy.

We need to build the foundation of our own happiness. Our spouse and children will add to it in different ways, but they are not primarily responsible for it. They can't be. As soon as we put the responsibility onto someone else, we become the victim of our own circumstance. A great marriage and raising children can add to your happiness and make life much more rewarding but that can't be the only source of our happiness. If we make it someone else's job to make us happy, aren't we more likely to be disappointed and become frustrated or depressed? Think about it, if I put too much emphasis on my children making me happy and they start to grow up and pursue their own lives and interests, what happens to my happiness then?

Many parents don't really know what to do with themselves as their children become more independent. All their happiness is wrapped up in what their children do; their sports; their passions. They may even start to delay the development of their child's independence and hold on too tightly because they are lost without that parenting role in their lives. This puts a lot of pressure on the child to fill this role and can even push the child away because they feel smothered. Even worse, the child may never fully pursue all that they could be because they can't pull away from their parents to make their own way. The way I see it is my spouse is my life partner, we do this life together, it is a great partnership but if I am waiting for him to "make me happy" I am asking him to do something that is impossible for him to do.

Making happiness your responsibility also means you let go of the expectations you put on others to "make" you happy. Unmet expectations create disappointment and resentment. Most of us aren't particularly good at even communicating our expectations of others so it is quite certain that we will be disappointed. If I place my happiness in the hands of those who don't even know what I need or want, I am on the fast track to unhappiness. As we learn to take responsibility for our own happiness, we must learn what we need or want, and learn to communicate it to those we love, in a healthy way. So many times, I have failed to communicate what I need or want, and then get so angry or disappointed when those expectations aren't met. Your family can't read your mind (even after 20 years of marriage)!

Here is an example I am certain all moms can relate to. It was my 11th Mother's Day. Over the years many Mother's Days have been sweet and wonderful, and my family has made me feel loved and appreciated. There have also been a few that were very disappointing. I was left wondering if there was any forethought or planning involved or if I was just an afterthought. Come on ladies, can I get an Amen? I am sure every mom has felt that way. That year was one of those years. It wasn't that it was totally overlooked but it was very last minute. When the whole city was looking for things to do with their moms on the same day, last minute, does not work very well. The next year, I noticed, as we once again approached that special day in May, I started to worry that it might happen again. I decided I didn't want to live in anticipation of disappointment, so I chose to proactively communicate what I needed to my spouse. I didn't make the plans for him and take over (like many of us do when we are disappointed), I just explained that I needed him to take the initiative and make sure there was a plan. That's an example of owning my happiness. I knew I needed them to make me feel special and important and so I asked for what I needed. This helped my husband be successful. He did a great job planning a nice breakfast out and finding a special gift (I might have hinted about what that should be) but I set him up to succeed instead of hoping he would figure it out somehow. Taking responsibility doesn't mean we don't need other people; it just means we aren't the victim of our circumstance. I wasn't going to be the victim of another poorly planned Mother's Day, so I took responsibility by communicating what I needed. In a perfect world, every husband or wife would know exactly what their spouse needs all the time but that's not the world we live in. Most of us struggle to find time to do everything we need to do every day, so we are likely to drop the ball occasionally. By taking responsibility for ourselves, we can support each other and give each other a better chance. We can have open communication about what is important and what isn't.

Change your perspective and take ownership of your own happiness. When you begin to feel neglected or forgotten, don't be a victim of your circumstance. Speak up, ask for what you need. I know it is vulnerable. What if they don't hear you? If you have been vulnerable by asking, and there is no response, it is even more difficult to handle the disappointment. Maybe that is the risk. We aren't willing to risk being disappointed. Of course, there are no guarantees that we will get the response we want but in my own life, I have realized that if I don't open up, I am likely to be disappointed anyway. Asking increases the odds and gives my spouse or my family a better idea of what is important to me. If you are in a loving family, I believe they will hear you and rise to the challenge. These open conversations give them insight into who you are. It helps them know you better. We think they should already know us but unless we are open and share what we need they will never really know us. Be vulnerable and have the courage to share what you need.

Now I know that some of you are not in a healthy relationship. Perhaps communicating and asking for what you need is not received very well or even heard. I must admit that this isn't my area of expertise. I realize that owning your happiness must be a bigger challenge. Perhaps it is even more important if you are in a less than perfect relationship. If your relationship with your spouse or children isn't that healthy then you need to be even more aware of what brings you joy and make sure you include more of it into your life. It is easy to blame someone else for not "making" you happy. It's more difficult to realize it is your own responsibility and start making changes. You need to learn to treat yourself well. Buy yourself a great birthday present. Something you really want that you would never 'waste' money on. Self-care is of the utmost importance when there isn't anyone else looking out for you. It isn't all about material things either, it could be taking a walk, a relaxing bubble bath, or going out for a great breakfast. Treat yourself well, you deserve it.

How do we own our happiness when we are disappointed by those we love? Human beings will always disappoint us. We are all so imperfect. If we attach our happiness to the actions of others, we are powerless. Remember, you disappoint the people you love, too. Chances are there is brokenness inside them that is unresolved. They are acting out of that brokenness even if they are not aware. Gratitude can make all the difference in these moments. Looking at the blessings in your life and meditating on all that God has given you. It may be a beautiful sunset or safe place to live. We all have many things to be thankful for and gratitude has a way of chasing out resentment and anger.

Let's begin the process of discovering a few things you could do that feed your happiness. When do you feel truly content and at peace? What activities can you really get lost in? What energizes you and brings you to life? Think about all areas of your life: your hobbies, volunteer work, music, arts, sports, your work. There may be parts of your work that you really love doing. Is there something you have always wanted to do or learn? Write down 10 things right now. **I'm serious, do not move on without writing 10 things down!** If you are struggling with this, then it is even more important to do it.

Now, how can you start weaving more of these things into your daily life? Choose 1 or 2 and strategize on how you can add it into your life. We tell ourselves we don't have time but if it is important, you will make time. There are many things we spend time doing that don't fill us or energize us. Things like TV and scrolling social media. We can spend hours a week on these time-wasting activities instead of doing something that we would really enjoy. Take a social media/Netflix vacation for a few weeks and see how much extra time you have. If you love music and dancing, plan a date night with your spouse at a restaurant that has live music. Dust off that old instrument and start playing again. Take one small step to incorporate just **one** new thing into your life. Commit to that step right now and take immediate action. Stop procrastinating and go to your schedule and book it in. If you schedule it, you will have time. You will plan around it. If you have young children and childcare is an issue, talk to your spouse about it. Maybe you can take turns and each take some time to do something for yourself. Work together and you will both have more to give to your family.

Ultimately happiness is a choice. It is a decision. Every day we get to choose what we focus on. It is a choice to focus on the shortcomings of the people in our lives or the problems we are facing. We can really lose ourselves in our problems, can't we? We all have problems and yours are not worse than everyone else's. We all like to think ours are worse but often they aren't. Think about it this way: if we all had to write our biggest problem down on a sheet of paper and we folded those papers up and put them all in a hat and then got to redraw which problem we would have, what would happen? Some of you would want your old problem back! I used to think that happy people didn't have problems or challenges in their lives. What I have since learned is that they do, they just choose to be happy anyway! **Happiness is not a problem free life; it is finding ways to be happy and content in the midst of the problems.**

Start to cultivate happiness in your life. Stop making excuses about why you don't do what you used to love to do anymore! Start choosing to do the things you love. Start having the experiences you want to have with the people you want to experience it with. Start communicating with those you love and let them know what is important to you. They might just surprise you!

– *chapter 10*

LET GOD HEAL YOUR HEART

I CAN'T WRITE a book on living abundantly without talking about your heart. It probably should have been one of the first chapters now that I think about it but I probably wasn't ready to be so vulnerable in the first few chapters. I know it isn't too late to have this part of the conversation that I know for sure. It will take some courage on my part but if it will help you have a more abundant life, I am up for it.

I discovered the healing power of the Holy Spirit in my 30's. I had two young children, a great career and a loving, devoted husband. Life was good, but I wasn't. Despite all these successes that I have encouraged you to pursue, I was still unhappy, there was this nagging doubt, this feeling of unworthiness and this shame that I carried everywhere. I was involved in my church a little bit; I was learning more about God through Bible studies. After years of ignoring God, I thought I was doing well but I couldn't shake the shame and doubt. I went through the motions of the "Christian Culture" - feeling unsettled and dissatisfied.

Then God found a way to reach me, and everything changed!

It started with a chance meeting at a children's park as we

watched our toddlers play. We became fast friends which was rare for me. I'm a natural introvert, so making new friends was difficult, but Christine was a bubbly extrovert that seemed so genuine and kind. I liked her right away. We got to know each other better and our friendship strengthened when we discovered we shared the same faith. We began talking about God and what we were learning in our bible studies.

Then one evening she told me about an incredible experience that she had. She had gone for prayer ministry with two ladies from her church. They had spent a few hours with her praying and ministering to her and she was healed emotionally from childhood bullying. As I listened to her explain how transformational this was, I could hear a voice in my head telling me to go see these praying women. I didn't know what prayer ministry was, all I knew is that I needed to go. My heart was pounding, and I was so scared. I couldn't even listen to all her story, there was so much going on in my own thoughts. I went home after our talk, and I knew I had to go see these ladies. I sent Christine a message late that night – so I wouldn't change my mind – and I asked her for their number. I am not even sure why I thought they would meet with me. Why would two strangers spend an afternoon with someone they didn't know trying to help her? The next day I called before I chickened out.

I knew why God was prompting me to go see these ladies. I needed emotional healing from something that happened to me as a young child. I was molested as a young girl by a teenage neighbour boy. I had never told anyone, maybe because the molester was a family friend, maybe because I felt so ashamed, maybe I thought it was my fault. I am not sure how long it went on but it was repetitive over a period of time. If I had to guess I would say I was about 5 or 6 years old. I didn't tell my older sisters, my mom or even a friend. It's the shame that convinces you to keep quiet and it is the silence that allows it to continue.

So here I was many, many years later in my 30s, successful, happily married, with the 2 little boys I had always dreamt of having and I should have been happy. But I wasn't... under all the success was a lingering doubt, a feeling of unworthiness, a deep shame. Despite years and years of personal development training, I couldn't shake the foundation of shame that was laid so long ago.

Somehow, I found the courage to walk through the door of Marg's home. There I met two amazing women of God that selflessly gave of their time to help people. There a life was restored and transformed because of their willingness to be used by God. They obeyed the call of God on their lives and allowed the Holy Spirit to use them. **That is what happens when you allow God to use you! Lives are changed!** Who could you reach and transform if you were listening and responding to the call of God on your life? Who could you pull out of the pit of shame and hopelessness? Imagine the possibilities.

The love of God flowed through Marg and Irene; I could see it in their eyes. Somehow, I knew this was a safe place to tell my story. You see when someone knows the Saviour, I mean really knows Him, His love shines through them, and people can see it. It's different than human love. It's a love that's so accepting, so complete, so safe.

After 30 years of silence, I told my deepest darkest secret to these women I had just met. They walked me through a process of compassionate listening. I connected with that defenceless, innocent 6-year-old little girl and for the first time realized it was not her fault. I saw what had happened through an accurate lens instead of the story my shame had made up. I cried for that sweet innocent 6-year-old girl for the first time. For 30 years, I had blamed her for what had happened and felt as if it was her fault.

Then they asked if I could forgive him... for the first time I had shifted all the blame onto the perpetrator and then they asked if I could forgive... He had stolen so much from me, my innocence, my self-worth. "No" I said, "I can't forgive." We kept on praying asking God to help me forgive. You see talking about what happened to me was not enough. Acknowledging the pain wasn't enough. **It's the forgiveness that sets us free.** Suddenly, I had the grace to forgive. It just shifted suddenly, and I knew I could do it. That's how God's grace works. He has this way of changing our hearts. In that moment everything changed! God healed the emotional wounds from so long ago and truly set me free. It was as complete, whole and transformational as the paralytic at the Beautiful Gate in Acts 3. If you could physically see the transformation, you would see it is as dramatically as a paralytic rising to his feet and dancing through the temple court!

Trauma like that cripples you emotionally. On the outside you look okay but inside you are broken. You try to convince yourself that it wasn't that big of a deal, others endure much more. This is true, many have endured much more than I did as a child but that doesn't mean that it wasn't damaging and wrong! **God wants to heal those wounds and make you whole so you can fully answer the call of God on your life and impact others.** A wounded soldier isn't as effective in God's army as a healthy, whole soldier.

If the story stopped there it would be a great story of victory over the enemy, but it doesn't stop there. Marg and Irene then asked me to pray silently and just let God speak to me. Just seek Him. In those few minutes three words came into my mind repeatedly. They asked me if anything had come into my mind while I was praying, any words that stood out to me. I hesitated, feeling self-conscious and unsure. I could only say 2 out of the 3 words.

Worthy
Clean
I was afraid to say the 3rd word because it was so uncomfortable for me.

Marg then left the room and suddenly Irene looked me right in the eye with tears running down her face and said, "You are so beautiful." A few minutes later Marg came back in and looked me square in the eyes and said, "You are so beautiful". Marg hadn't heard what Irene had said. God had put that on their heart to say. It wasn't them saying it, it was God. The 3rd word that God had said to me was "Beautiful" I didn't believe it so I couldn't even say it out loud to them. God wanted to make sure that I knew he had said it. How great is our God? How much does He care for us? He was not letting me leave that place without knowing what He said. I never felt so loved by God as I did in that moment. It washed away all the doubt, unworthiness, and shame.

I praise you because I am fearfully and wonderfully made; your works are wonderful, I know that full well. Psalm 139:14 NIV

Everything changed between God and me that day. He went from a God up there, distant, watching from afar to a God that knows me better than I know myself. A God that cares so individually for me, not just the world globally, but me as an individual. A God that desires wholeness and healing for the broken-hearted. I came to know God in a whole new way that day. He literally made me whole that day. He healed that old wound that I had carried for so long. Just like the paralytic at the Beautiful Gate I wanted to jump and leap and praise my GOD!

So he, leaping up, stood and walked and entered the temple with them- walking, leaping, and praising God. Acts 3:8 NIV

Such a joyful picture, the lame leaping up! That is what happened to my heart that day! It was made whole by the power of the Holy Spirit.

You too can be made new by the power of the Holy Spirit. You may not have been molested as a child, but you may have been betrayed or hurt in other ways, perhaps your trauma is much worse. These experiences create heart wounds and bitter roots that change who we are and keep us from living the full, abundant lives that God desires for us. A pastor once told me that God had given her a picture of God's people, the army of God, but all the soldiers were wounded. An army filled with wounded soldiers is not that effective. God needs an army of people that are strong emotionally to fight the battle. For that to happen, our hearts need to be whole.

Three things happened at Marg's home that day.

First, God healed the heart of that 6-year-old girl, I saw how much it grieved God that this happened to me, it broke his heart. Through prayer and the Holy Spirit, God was able to go back and heal that little girl, He restored my brokenness. God's love is so perfect, He invaded my heart and I was made whole in that moment.

Secondly, God helped me forgive the person who hurt me. Unforgiveness keeps us bound up in chains. This gave me freedom from the bitterness and anger. I used to hate the man who did this to me. Hating him wasn't hurting that man, it was hurting me. It was keeping me locked up in pain. I could only forgive through the power of the Holy Spirit. I could not forgive him on my own. Forgiveness is not saying that what the person did was okay, it is choosing to let go of the hate and bitterness so you can heal and be free.

Shortly after Kathy died, I had a vivid dream that I believe was a message from God. In the dream I had surgery in the area around my heart or chest. Something was removed by the surgery. After the surgery I was at a family event and my uncles and cousins were asking me what the surgery was for. All I could say was that they removed something black and dark from me. The dream initially scared me, I wondered "Is this a warning from God that I have cancer?" I started praying and asked God to show me the meaning of this dream. A peace came over me and I knew it wasn't a warning. God was trying to show me that unforgiveness leaves something dark in our hearts and God wants to do 'heart surgery' and remove it. He wants to heal our hearts so we can be whole and fully functioning for his Kingdom. This is why I have the courage to tell my story. I believe God wants to heal more hearts and if my story just helps one person have the courage to face what happened to them and seek God for healing then it is worth the vulnerability. If it gives one person the strength to forgive those who betrayed and hurt them, it is worth it. I have a strong belief today that unforgiveness is the source of so much pain. I believe it can actually make us physically sick not just emotionally sick. The mind, body and spirit are so connected. God wants his people to be whole, strong and mighty. Able to do the work of the Kingdom. Forgiveness is one way to strengthen his army.

Lastly, God restored my identity. The trauma had changed my identity. I could not believe that I was worthy and beautiful. I had spent most of my life feeling dirty and unclean. He restored his identity of who I was created to be. Knowing who you are in Christ is key to an abundant life. God could not let me leave Marg's home without restoring my identity. I left that home a new person, feeling confident and sure of who I am in Christ. Knowing my identity in Christ changed my whole world.

I believe you are reading this book for a reason; it is not an accident. Perhaps, there is something in your past that you need

God's supernatural healing for or perhaps someone you know is in need. I encourage you to seek God's help. If you are not sure where to go to get the help, there are organizations that have developed Holy Spirit led ways of helping people. The one I am most familiar with is called Elijah House but there are many. **Please check out the resource page at the end of the book to learn more and find help.** I know seeking help can be so scary and vulnerable, but your freedom is on the other side of that fear. People may have even made you feel that your issues are too big and complicated to overcome. That is a lie of the enemy and you need to stop believing it. Perhaps it is too complicated for people but nothing is too complicated for God! Let's pray for the wisdom and courage to seek the help we need.

We cry out to you Abba father, you know our deepest pain. You know the shame and unworthiness that we hold deep in our hearts. You know who has hurt us and the damage it has done to our mind, body and spirit. Lord, give us the courage to take the first step toward healing. Connect us with those who can help. Help us find your people that believe in your Holy Spirit and your power to heal us and set us free. – Amen

I believe God is so excited to show you what He has planned for you on the other side of that pain and fear. Healing your heart and learning to forgive is an important part of living abundantly. Take the first step, just like a toddler taking their first steps, you will feel uncertain and nervous. **Let the vision of being fully whole and able to live in the abundance of Christ lead you.** It is worth it, for soon you will be free to walk and run living abundantly through Christ! I know that full well, my friend.

— *chapter 11*

GOD INTENDED
IT FOR GOOD

> *You intended to harm me but God intended it for good to accomplish what is now being done, the saving of many lives.*
> Genesis 50:20 NIV

IT'S BEEN SAID by many "Everything happens for a reason". This helps us make sense of this broken world when bad or difficult things happen. Implied in this statement is the idea that God somehow orchestrates these bad events so he can turn them around and use them for good. Honestly, this has never made much sense to me. I have wondered "How can a good and loving God orchestrate bad things upon his people?" Let's just consider an example; a child gets a rare, incurable disease and it is terminal. After struggling to treat it and find a cure, the child passes away. The family donates the child's body to medical research and because of that research a treatment is found, and many children are saved. You could say "Everything happens for a reason, because of her death many were saved." That sounds lovely and romantic unless you are the mother or father of that child. Wouldn't you ask God why your child was chosen to die for the cause? That would be difficult to reconcile. Did God really mean to harm their child? Was he the author of that sickness? I don't believe He was. Everything God created was found to be exceptionally good. (See Genesis 1:31) Sickness and disease were not a part of His plan, not part of the Garden of Eden. It wasn't until sin entered the world that we even had sickness and disease. What I believe is that sometimes people mean to do us harm and sometimes satan means to do us harm and I believe God takes those acts, as horrible and destructive as they are, and finds a way to turn it around for good.

It takes us acting on it to accomplish the good. We are partners, co-labourers, with Him so we must be willing participants.

"For we are God's fellow workers..." 1 Corinthians 3:9 NIV

He wants to partner with us to use it for good. I believe He gives us the opportunity to use it for good but often we are so filled with bitterness and anger that we don't take the opportunity. Imagine the good in the world if we all listened to that still small voice prompting us to use it for good. Wouldn't that be a healthier way to grieve and honour those that we have lost? To create something good, in partnership with the creator, because of what was lost. I also think of this as the ultimate revenge on satan. I must admit that is a bit of a motivator for me. I think I have caused him some frustration and anger because I won't fall into the pit of despair when bad things happen. Instead, I look for ways to positively influence the world and help others. That must really annoy satan, don't you think? Once again, the words of Joanne Clancy come to mind to keep me going,

"Be the kind of woman that when your feet hit the floor in the morning the devil says "Oh no, she's up."

Of course, I am not saying we all don't need time to grieve or process what happens to us but if we get stuck there then God can't use it for good.

I know God didn't want me to be sexually abused as a child, and he certainly did not orchestrate it. In fact, I am sure he tried to stop the person who did it, and was unsuccessful. God can't supersede our will. He can try to influence us by telling us it is wrong, but we often ignore his voice when he tries to correct us. Through his Holy Spirit he can also try to influence those around us by prompting them to do something. It may be by giving them an uneasy feeling about the person, situation or prompting them to go somewhere for no apparent reason. Unfortunately, we often don't act when God nudges us this way, we brush it off or think it is silly. I believe God often gives a solution to stop what is happening, but sometimes we are too afraid to act on it. We worry about being rejected or judged or alone and don't follow the solution that God is giving us, and as a result suffer more than we should. Hebrews 5:11 says *We have much to say about this, but it is hard to make it clear to you because you no longer try to understand.* In our pain, we may stop trying to understand and shut out God. This is one reason why we should learn to hear His voice and know Him more so that when He prompts us, we know to act. The habit of hearing his voice and acting in obedience is so important.

> *"My sheep listen to my voice; I know them, and they follow me." John 10:27 NIV*

I have no doubt that God was acting on my behalf in many ways, trying to stop what was happening. There is no way to know but perhaps it would have continued much longer or would have gone further if he hadn't. What I do remember is the family moved away. I am not sure why, but I thank God that they did and it all ended.

Since the day that God healed my heart from the sexual abuse, God has been using it for all kinds of good. He has given me so many opportunities to introduce people to Him because they have gone through similar trauma. He has given me opportunity to introduce other Christians to the supernatural healing power of God to heal their hearts as well. That's a chance for people to get free of the damage that the trauma has caused, heal their heart and live more fully. It has also given me an empathy that people sense and they open up to me for no reason. They tell me things that they have never told anyone. God is using that trauma to help others and it is truly a beautiful thing. What we receive from God, we can freely give to others. 2 Corinthians 1:3-4 describes it so perfectly,

Praise be to the God and Father of our Lord Jesus Christ, the Father of compassion and the God of all comfort, who comforts us in all our troubles, so that we can comfort those in any trouble with the comfort we ourselves receive from God.

God has done such amazing work through that childhood trauma that I have come to be thankful for it. I realize that sounds crazy and it is difficult to believe. If I hadn't had that experience, I wouldn't have reached out to God the way I did and had such a powerful encounter with God. I wouldn't have come to know Him the way that I did. My relationship with God would have continued to be superficial. Experiencing the healing power of God in a such a dramatic way has changed everything for me. I started to realize that if He could heal one trauma then He can heal other inner hurts that were holding me back. Over the next few years, I worked through many of the inner wounds of my childhood and teen years with the help of different ministries and Holy Spirit filled believers. I am a completely different person as a result. I found full freedom as I discovered the fullness of His love and realized my identity in Him.

> *Rejoice always, pray continually, give thanks in all circumstances; for this is God's will for you in Christ Jesus. 1 Thessalonians 5:16-18 NIV*

If you study the word, you can see many examples of this principle at work. The story of Jesus' crucifixion being one of them. Jesus went to the cross which was meant to harm Him. He was tortured, humiliated and ultimately killed in a way that would be considered very inhumane today. But what was meant to harm Him ultimately allowed Him to accomplish his mission here on earth, the saving of many lives. They didn't realize they were playing right into the divine plan of God to save us from our sin. God used the people that were against Jesus to accomplish what he wanted to accomplish through him.

Losing my sister was the hardest thing I have ever had to walk through. Losing someone you love is always difficult but losing someone to cancer is particularly heart-breaking. Watching someone you love endure such suffering is so incredibly painful. It could have been an event that rocked my faith to its core but instead it has refined my faith. It matured it and made my faith stronger than it ever was. Like the melting down of gold to purify and refine it, our trials refine our faith. There are many verses in the bible about the refiner's fire.

> *This third I will put into the fire; I will refine them like silver and test them like gold. They will call on my name and I will answer them; I will say, 'They are my people,' and they will say, 'The LORD is our God.'" Zechariah 13:9 NIV*

I am sure the enemy meant to cause doubt in my heart and destroy my faith. Instead, it was a catalyst. I wanted to pass the test and come out on the other side saying, "This is my God!" I realized that if I lost faith and shrank back from the life God has planned for me, then the enemy really does win and have victory. You see the enemy had no victory when Kathy passed away either. Jesus took care of that on the cross! She has everlasting life in Him. Only if I chose to get bitter and angry at the cancer or at God, only then would the enemy be victorious. Choosing instead to use it as a catalyst to yield my life to God and live the best life that I can is another way to defeat the enemy. Losing Kathy, made me realize that life really is short and you just don't know how long you have to make the impact that God wants you to make in the world. I may only have 5 or 10 or 50 years left. We aren't guaranteed anything on this earth. If I only have 5 or 10, they are going to count! I am going to make an impact for God on the people I reach. I am not going to waste the time that God gives me. I am going to enjoy my family, have great experiences and help as many people as possible to know God; His power to heal their hearts and bodies; and His great love for them. I allowed this terrible experience to create such a sense of urgency, one that I never had before. I try not to take time or people for granted as much as I used to. I may not have another chance to tell them about Jesus. I may not have another chance to get the message of living abundantly out to them. If you want to know the value of time, ask someone who has lost someone they love. What would be the value of one more day with them? Death changes how you live. It changes your perspective; what you value.

The choice is ours; we choose to allow God to use it for good or choose not to. God gave us free will. We are co-labourers, remember. He can use it if we surrender it to him; if we seek Him amid our grief and anger. Often bitterness and anger get in the way. When we are so bitter and angry, it's difficult for God to work in our lives. Now I understand that it is very normal to feel angry with God when something bad happens. I felt that way too. I was so disappointed in Him when my sister passed away. It was overwhelming. It's very normal to have those feelings, but if we allow those feelings to take over our hearts long term, and never deal with them, then we put up walls around our hearts that shut God out. It's more difficult for God to work in our lives if we shut Him out. I almost used the word impossible, but nothing is impossible for our God. He will keep trying regardless of what we do. He is like the shepherd that leaves the ninety-nine sheep to go find the one lost sheep.

> *"Suppose one of you has a hundred sheep and loses one of them. Doesn't he leave the ninety-nine in the open country and go after the lost sheep until he finds it? And when he finds it, he joyfully puts it on his shoulders and goes home. Then he calls his friends and neighbours together and says, 'Rejoice with me; I have found my lost sheep.' Luke 15:4-6 NIV*

He will not give up on us. Yes, we can slow the process down with our walls of anger and bitterness, unless we learn to forgive and let go; allowing God to heal our hurts and use it for good. I allowed my sister's death to refine my faith, I allowed God to use it. Now don't get me wrong, I questioned God and when I was questioning Him, I heard Him say "I will use this to refine your faith." I was so full of doubt and grief in that moment, I couldn't see how it would refine my faith, but I chose to believe it anyway. I made a decision that day. I decided to allow it to refine my faith. I decided to ask the hard questions that were coming up about Him. I went to my spiritual leaders and asked. No question was off limits. I chose not to isolate myself from God and my spiritual family even though I was tempted to. It would have been easier to stay angry in the moment. It would have been less work and I would have felt less vulnerable. Admitting that something has rocked your faith is not easy. I wanted to declare to the world that "Death has no victory!" but that was not how I felt. It felt like God had abandoned us on the battlefield. Choosing to allow it to refine my faith was not an easy choice. It went against everything my humanity wanted in that moment. Choosing to believe God in the middle of the pain made all the difference.

This opened the door for God to use it for good.

– *chapter 12* –

BUT I AM NOT STRONG ENOUGH

I AM NOT a gambling woman, but if I had to bet on one thing, I would bet that as you've been reading through this book, you have had this thought run through your mind, "I am not strong enough to live this abundant life." I know it sounds exciting and full, but it also sounds hard. It sounds challenging and vulnerable. I won't lie to you, it is. If I had to rely on my strength alone, I would never be able to walk this path. Can I tell you a little secret? The fear of not being strong enough was my #1 fear in this whole journey. I put off my best life for years because I didn't feel strong enough to live at that level. I didn't think I could handle it at all. I stayed at a level I knew I could handle; it was nice and safe, and it didn't require me to rely on God. I was successful enough to receive a few accolades occasionally, but I was not walking in the fullness of what God wanted me to do, not even close. I was doing just enough to justify that I was more courageous than most. But the Bible doesn't say, "I came that you may have a better than average life," does it? No, I am sorry, but that is not what it says. *It says, "I came that you may have life, and have it abundantly!"*

Now this doesn't mean I have completely mastered the gravitational pull of my comfort zone. I am not sure that you can ever completely master it. It will always pull at you, tempting you back into your cosy old life where you didn't take chances or overcome fear. Occasionally you will slip back into it like a nice comfortable pair of pyjamas and that is ok. We all need times of rest and recuperation. **But just like our pyjamas, we can't wear them every day and we aren't meant to live in our comfort zones all the time either.** We are designed to be challenged and grow. This is what produces character, perseverance, and strength. It opens the door to God using us in remarkable ways for His Kingdom. We must push ourselves beyond what we believe we can do, to where we need Him to help us. If you are 100% certain you can do it on your own, you aren't thinking BIG enough. Think bigger. Have a vision big enough that you need HIS help. That's where you are supposed to go.

Now I am sure if you didn't believe in God, and didn't have the power of the Holy Spirit to help you out, you could somehow muster up the strength to do this on your own. I mean non-believers do it all the time, don't they? But here is the great news – **you don't have to!** I am so thankful for this. **We have the assistance of the King of Kings at our disposal and most of us aren't using it.** We are trying to do everything on our own, with our resources and it slows us down and makes it a long hard road. I am not saying it is going to be easy just because you decide to rely on His strength. You will experience challenges and discomfort but somehow you will be better able to handle them. You will have more grace for it. Your capacity to grow and achieve will increase when you choose to let Him be your strength and not just your own will power.

Tapping into His strength also reduces stress. So much of our stress comes from striving to achieve on our own, outside of His grace. When I am tapped into His strength, I find myself accomplishing more with what feels like less effort. It isn't that magical things happen without effort, but it feels like less effort. The load isn't as heavy and it's not as difficult. Meditate on this verse,

"I can do all things through Christ who gives me strength."
Philippians 4:13 NKJV

This verse became my lifeline when I felt so overwhelmed with raising my young children and the leadership responsibilities I had in my business. Every time the overwhelm threatened to overtake me like a wave crashing on the shore, I repeated that verse, over and over. It reminded me that He didn't call me into these roles and then abandon me to figure it out. He was with me, equipping me and guiding me.

Our strength is limited, His is infinite. Tap into the infinite strength of God! When I feel too weak to do all He has called me to do this verse becomes my battle cry. It reminds me that it isn't my strength that is needed. He will provide all I need. He provides the strength, the strategy, the ideas, and the resources. His resources are infinite. Who am I to doubt the plans of God in my life?

And this same God who takes care of me will supply all your needs from his glorious riches, which have been given to us in Christ Jesus. Philippians 4:19 NLT

Paul says this to the Philippians after they send him provisions to take care of him. They had set their focus on others and, in return, God promises to take care of them. Their focus wasn't on their needs, they saw Paul's need and provided for him. The result was the promise that God would take care of their needs.

Isn't that beautiful? **If we take our eyes off ourselves and our limitations and meditate instead on the good that we can do in the world, He will provide all we need according to HIS riches in glory.** Now we like to read this and think this is a financial promise, and it very well could be financial, but we should consider what else could be considered His riches. He is rich in many other ways. Rich in peace, love, mercy, rest, strength, and power.

I'm sure you could add a few more blessings to that list.

Now I'm not sure if there were a few words that jumped out at you like they did at me when I reread that verse. These two small words grabbed my attention "His riches". According to His riches, now that's exciting! Not according to your riches or mine but HIS! Here we are trying to supply our own needs according to our riches which if you haven't noticed are limited at times. All we see are the limitations of our riches so we are filled with doubt about what we can accomplish. What Paul is telling the Philippians is that God is now supplying all their needs according to His riches. That's a much better source to rely on. **If I'm going to rely on any source, I choose the God of unlimited resources thank you very much!** But we must take our eyes off ourselves long enough to see what God is calling us to do. We need to start seeking Him instead of comfort.

Grace is defined as being empowered by God. This is what happens when you choose to rely on His strength. He empowers you to do what He is calling you to do. Most people spend so much time worrying about how they will accomplish what they are wanting to accomplish, that time could be used differently. Instead of worrying, we could meditate on what God could do to help. The worrying stops the creative process, it blocks the flow of ideas. It blocks God. What would happen if we finally accepted that we are going to do what we are supposed to do, and trusted that God would give us the wisdom to do it? Would

God really give us an assignment and not give us any tools to complete it? The word says,

> *The Lord makes firm the steps of the one who delights in him; though he may stumble, he will not fall, for the Lord upholds him with his hand. Psalm 37:23-24 NIV*

He makes firm the steps of the one who delights in Him. If you are running from His plans in your life, worrying about how it will all work, would you consider that to be 'delighting in Him'? It is like you are having a giant argument with the Lord! When my children argue with me, it is not delightful! He is pulling on your heartstrings and whispering in your ear the great and wonderful things He needs you to do, and you are mentally running through a list of reasons why you can't do it. That doesn't seem delightful to me. Delight in Him. Come to Him with an open heart believing all things are possible with God. Then wait and listen for instruction. Delight in what He has placed in you and the gifts He has given you and approach Him with faith that He will make your steps firm.

If we are seeking Him in what we are doing and letting him lead us, I believe that He will uphold us and not let us fall. We may stumble but even when we make a mistake or go in a wrong direction, he will lead us back to the right path, if we allow Him to.

I did a Google search on verses that speak about God directing our steps. One source had 64 verses on that topic! 64! and that is just one source. Now I didn't have time to cross reference the other sources but wow, isn't that exciting? Why are we so filled with doubt about our future? We should be waking up every morning thanking and praising him for directing our steps.

> *Trust in the Lord with all your heart, and do not lean on your own understanding. In all your ways acknowledge Him and he will make straight your paths. Proverbs 3:5 - 6 ESV*

These verses rock me to the core. **Are we trusting him with ALL our hearts or worrying with all our hearts?** We try to use logic and human understanding to find our way, but the Lord says, *"Do not lean on your own understanding"* Who should we be leaning on? On God! Where should we be seeking answers? And if we do seek Him and lean on His understanding and trust him, what does he say will happen? He will make our paths straight. The shortest distance between two points is a straight line. What he is saying is that his way is the shortest way, but it may not be the most logical way. It may not even seem like the right way sometimes. Think about the walls of Jericho. I mean that took some real faith to follow His instructions. Walk around this heavily fortified double wall for 7 days and blow some trumpets. Yes, that sounds like a great way to attack a heavily fortified city. Let's be honest, it is completely crazy. But the walls came tumbling down because they were obedient. They followed his instructions, not their own.

Now, the Israelites weren't always this obedient. What happened when they did their own thing? They wandered in the wilderness for 40 years and missed out on the promised land! Sources say the journey could have been completed in 11 days, yet it took them 40 years. The Lord even led them on a longer route because he knew their mindset wasn't strong enough yet. In Exodus 13:17 it says,

> *When Pharaoh let the people go, God did not lead them on the road through the Philistine country, though that was shorter. For God said, "If they face war, they might change their minds and return to Egypt." NIV*

The Lord knew, after years of slavery, they weren't strong enough to stand strong in battle. He knew their fear and doubt might cause them to run back to what they were comfortable with in Egypt. He knew they might sacrifice their freedom for comfort and safety. How many of us miss our promised land because we are wandering in the wilderness of doubt and worry, taking the "safe and secure" path to nowhere? When you read your bible, what happens when his people follow His instructions? Miraculously amazing rescues and provision. It leaves me wondering, why do we doubt so much? Why have we forgotten who our God is? Perhaps we neglect reading our Bible, so we have forgotten how great our God is. Perhaps we haven't forgotten the story but just lack the revelation to apply it to our lives. These stories are there to show us the greatness of our God and to show us what happens when we wander aimlessly doing it our way and what happens when we obey God. Do we read these stories for entertainment only or to apply them to our own lives? What would happen if we allowed the story to show us who our God is and how amazing his love and provision is for us?

The question we should be asking ourselves about our calling and future isn't "Am I strong enough?" The question really is "Am I obedient enough?" That is a better question. "Am I willing to do what He asks me to do even when it doesn't make logical sense?" He promises to direct your steps. Stand strong in his word. The bible says,

> *I will instruct you and teach you in the way you should go; I will counsel you with my eye upon you. Psalm 32:8 ESV*

Do you believe his promise? If you do, then you can trust that His way is the best way. The word says His eye is upon you.

He hasn't left you alone. He is watching just like good parents watch over their young child at play, allowing the child to try new things without interfering but ever so careful to intervene to prevent a bad injury. He is watching over us. We do not need to be afraid.

We can trust the Lord to give us instructions,

And your ears shall hear a word behind you, saying "This is the way, walk in it," when you turn to the right or turn to the left. Isaiah 30:21 ESV

He has promised to direct your steps. We can move forward in confidence, not confidence in ourselves, but confidence in the one who is calling us and directing our steps. This verse makes me picture someone moving along a path and the Lord behind them guiding them. I believe we must be in motion to be directed. We cannot stay still and wait. Just like we must put our car in drive and move before we can steer it. Have you ever tried to steer a stationary car? It's impossible, you can't move the steering wheel until you are in motion. The Lord cannot guide our steps until we start to move. That is why it is important to get started. You may not know exactly where you are going yet, but get started, give the Lord the chance to show you. There is great adventure ahead!

Many get caught up in how they are going to do what God wants them to do. They want all the steps upfront, all at once. A fully detailed description with all the steps laid out to follow. We want to understand it all before we jump into it. I understand that feeling. The craving for certainty and clarity. My observation is that it rarely works this way unless your calling is to open a McDonald's franchise, for a few million dollars you can get a step-by-step manual to run that business. For most of us, that isn't what we are called to do, and the process isn't as clearly laid out. Many will falter at this stage, give up and run back to their comfort zone. We want certainty and clarity, but God is asking us to have faith and trust Him. If it was so clearly laid out it would not take faith. God wants to develop our faith and teach us to trust Him. We want Him to connect all the dots before we start so we know what we are building but like a dot-to-dot puzzle we must start before the picture is revealed. If we refuse to start until we know what we are drawing, we will never begin and never see the picture. Our journey into His calling is much the same. We must take a few steps in faith before He reveals the next steps.

Trying to figure out the big picture too early can cause us to miss where He is taking us. We can get too attached to where we think He is taking us and miss his direction. We end up starting where He wanted us to start but then taking it where we want to take it instead of letting Him lead the way. We end up off track and missing where He is taking us. His viewpoint is different than ours. He knows where we need to develop and where we need to grow and get stronger. He knows how He needs to prepare us for the future. Let that sink in. **Your God knows you so intimately that He knows exactly where he needs to strengthen you before he can take you to your promised land.** What may seem like a detour or a stall, can be what is preparing you for what is coming in the future. We get frustrated when we are stalling or off track but that is because we are holding onto our preconceived ideas of where God is taking us. He may be using the detour to prepare us for what is ahead. If we submit to His way and not our way, then He can use it to take us where He wants us to go. **When you are frustrated and wondering why you are stuck, surrender it to Him asking Him to teach you through it, change you through it, make you stronger through it.** Lay it at the foot of the cross and let Him work through it. In surrender, He can lead us and direct our steps, whispering in our ear, go this way or that way.

When we try to figure it all out on our own, we miss the process that He wants to take us through. It's no wonder that we feel like we aren't strong enough! He isn't asking us to be superhuman without Him. He is asking us to tap into the supernatural power He provides through the Holy Spirit to do all that He asks us to do. All things are possible with Him who gives us strength. That's my secret to success. Tapping into the supernatural power of the King of Kings. With Him I am able. With Him I can overcome every challenge and obstacle. His wisdom directs my steps. His grace empowers. I will run and not grow weary. I will soar on wings like eagles.

> *But those who hope in the Lord will renew their strength. They will soar on wings like eagles; they will run and not grow weary; they will walk and not be faint. Isaiah 40:31 NIV*

Where do we place our hope? Our hope is in the Lord. If our hope is in our ability, we will tire more easily and retreat. Those who hope in the Lord will renew their strength. If our hope is in our talent, our work ethic, or our actions, eventually we tire or stall. Our hope is God, the maker of heaven and earth. If He can do all that, surely, he can and will help you! When we hope in the Lord, what happens? We soar, we run, we walk. We don't always go the same pace. There are seasons of soaring, when our success seems effortless, like an eagle gliding across the sky. Have you ever watched an eagle soar? It seems so effortless, it's incredible. It doesn't seem like he is striving to soar but certainly he is soaring. There will be times on your journey where your success feels effortless too.

There are also seasons of running. I took up running for a

season, I was committed, I loved it but it was short lived. The high impact nature of running isn't a great fit with my body, so I gave it up. I plan on spending a lot of time on this planet and I need this earthly body of mine to hold up until the end. What do these seasons of running look like? Running takes more effort than soaring, it was never effortless for me, perhaps a more dedicated runner would say otherwise but for most people running takes a lot of effort. Forcing yourself to go faster than what is comfortable takes will and effort. There are times when you will have to run, you will need to put in extra effort into achieving all that he is calling you to. You will need to push yourself and put in that effort but not grow weary. That's an exciting promise. You will be able to do more than you think you can, I promise! You will be able to go faster at times than you think you can. This was one of the biggest struggles I faced! Trust me, I am an expert on the topic. "I'm not strong enough" ran my life!

The word also promises *"You will walk and not faint."* There are seasons where the pace will be slower but steady. While walking you are still making progress, still moving forward at a steady pace. These are the seasons where the Lord allows you to recover. This might be a strategic time when you are preparing for the next sprint. It may be a time of creativity and imagination. A time for new ideas and directions. These seasons are important too. Seek the Lord in this time and he will keep preparing and guiding you.

I hope this inspires you to seek His strength. Ask his Holy Spirit to empower you to do all that you imagine. You can do ALL things with Christ who gives you strength! ALL THINGS! Not everything at once but nothing is off limits as far as what is possible.

For with God nothing shall be impossible

Luke 1:37 KJV says *For with God nothing shall be impossible.* Also, go and look at a few different translations. It's interesting how each translation words it a bit differently. Most translations include the words "with God" but a few have changed it to "for God". That seems to change the meaning quite a lot. Luke 1:26-38 recounts the time when the angel Gabriel visits Mary to tell her that she will become pregnant with Jesus. She is a virgin so believes that is impossible, of course. But with the power of the Holy Spirit nothing is impossible! The Lord had sent Gabriel to tell Mary. The Lord needed Mary to bring His son into the world fully man and fully God. He needed a woman to co-labour (no pun intended) with Him on his divine plan to save us. It was Mary "with God" and something impossible happened. **We are not called to walk alone. We are called to co-labour, to be empowered by the Holy Spirit to do all that we can ask or imagine.**

Ephesians 3:20 says *Now to him who is able to do immeasurably more than all we ask or imagine, according to his power that is at work within us.* I need to correct my last statement. I apologize. **IMMEASURABLY MORE THAN YOU CAN ASK OR IMAGINE.** If you think you are thinking big or have some grandiose plan, I know His plan is bigger and better. He hasn't revealed it all to you yet and He still thinks that you think too small! Let yourself ask and let yourself imagine! You might as well, His plan is immeasurably more than that anyway and that means it is possible. Let that sink in... Immeasurably more. That means it is bigger than you can measure. Bigger than you can think. That is God's abundant life for you!

Now I recognize that for some Christians this idea will make you very uncomfortable. You have always believed that Christians should stay humble and meek and not shine too brightly. The idea that you should ask God for anything seems arrogant. You shouldn't ask for too much or expect too much. I understand these feelings and beliefs, but I also want to challenge them a little. This is not about selfish ambition; it is about living the life that God wants you to live. It is about seeking His will for your life. **It is about surrendering your plans at the foot of the cross and allowing him to rearrange and transform them.** All of this takes humility. It takes the realization that your plans are not better than his. It is about putting all your trust in him, trusting that his wisdom and his path is truly what is best for you. I am convinced that God wants you to shine FOR HIM; not for earthly glory but for his kingdom. Let's read Psalm 45:3-5,

> *Gird your sword on your side, you mighty one;*
> *clothe yourself with splendour and majesty.*
> *In your majesty ride forth victoriously*
> *in the cause of truth, humility and justice;*
> *let your right hand achieve awesome deeds.*
> *Let your sharp arrows pierce the hearts of the king's enemies;*
> *let the nations fall beneath your feet.*

In humility, seek his wisdom and his plan for your life. Sometimes the world defines humility as diminished self-confidence. Alternatively, let's ask what is biblical humility? I found this definition on https://gentlechristianparenting.com and it resonates with me:

> *Biblical humility* **means believing what God says about you over anyone else's opinion, including your own.** *It requires embracing who you are in Christ over who you are in the flesh. To be biblically humble is to* **be so free of concern for your own ego that you unreservedly elevate those around**

you. With confidence and boldness, pursue the best that he has planned for you.

Truly seeking God's will for our lives and following him requires us to put our ego and our consideration for what people think aside in true humility. It is caring more about what God thinks you should do than what people think you should do. It is considering first what God wants, not what you want. It is walking in reverence of God, seeking to do what he desires. Proverbs 22:4 NIV says *Humility is the fear of the Lord; its wages are riches and honour and life.* Abundant life!

My friends, *do not throw away your confidence, for it will be richly rewarded.* (Hebrews 10:35 NIV) You are strong enough, good enough and deserving enough to live this abundant life in Christ. For in his strength, nothing is impossible! You are not walking this road alone; He is with you. He guides you and encourages you all the way. Step into the abundant life he has for you and experience immeasurably more than you can ask or imagine!

– chapter 13 –

AS HE SPEAKS

My sheep listen to my voice; I know them, and they follow me.
John 10:27 NIV

THE LORD WANTS us to hear his voice and follow Him. If we have a personal relationship with God, it involves listening for his voice and being obedient to it. I am thankful that I found a group of believers that were taught to listen for the word of God and deliver it to his people. The Lord is speaking to these people trained to hear His voice. He is speaking to all of us but often we miss it. A few of these people are courageous enough to speak the word out loud so it can build up and expand the faith, belief, and vision of God's people. If you can, find a group of believers that are tuned into God's voice. It can strengthen you as you learn to live abundantly. It isn't that he doesn't speak directly to you, he does, but we must be tuned into Him to hear it. Most of us are taught to pray, say a few words to God daily, thank Him for this, ask Him for that and say amen. Now that is good, but I want to suggest that something is missing. Are we taught to seek His presence, not His miracles, not His answers but simply His presence? Most of us need to be taught this. Taught to slow it down and set everything aside and just seek Him. Clearing your mind of all your tasks, responsibilities and needs. Just focusing solely on His presence. Like a lingering embrace where you just enjoy being together. The best way I can explain it is to compare it to how it feels when your young child crawls onto your lap and just leans against you. You don't say anything or do anything, you just hold each other, enjoying each other's presence. That's what seeking His presence is like for me. Just being with Him, not to request something, or even to pray about something, but just to linger in His presence.

When you learn to hear His voice, God will start to speak through you to encourage His people.

Over the last few years, I have received words of prophecy that have given me direction about what I am supposed to be doing and it has made a big difference. Sometimes the word confirms what is already a desire in your heart and sometimes it is a completely new direction.

The word that confirms what I have already been pondering or pursuing is easy to act on. What is more difficult is when I've received those words of prophecy that have revealed new paths. Writing was one of those new paths that was revealed to me and was completely unexpected. When I received that word, it was clearly from God, as it wasn't a secret desire of my heart. It wasn't something I was secretly wishing for but too scared to admit. What was fascinating to me was that as soon as it was spoken, something stirred in me, and I just knew "Yes that's it!" It scared me, I was uncertain, but I knew it was the truth. Now it would have been easy in that moment to keep the word hidden and pretend that it didn't ring true in my heart. I could have gone on with my plans, that all made sense in my little world, and wouldn't have had to complicate it with another pursuit. That would have been the easy, safe, more comfortable option. But it wouldn't be what God wants for me or what God needs me to do for His kingdom. After I received that word, I chose to tell some trusted friends. A few of them were there when I received it and heard it but if I didn't talk about after they likely would have forgotten. By acknowledging the impact it had on me, I now became accountable. I now have people in my life that know what I am called to do, and they won't let me forget it. That is a very good thing. It is so easy to hear what God is saying and then life gets in the way (and it always will) and you allow yourself to give up or ignore it completely. Pretending you didn't hear the word, doesn't change the fact that you did. I believe we will be held accountable for the assignments that God has for us. Will his words for us be "Well done good and faithful servant"? I realize that most of us will fall short in some area of our lives. There is unlimited potential in all of us but also limiting beliefs in all of us. It is quite likely that all of us will have some area or areas where we miss the mark of what God has planned. I just don't want to miss it all! I want to get as close as I can to what He has planned. I want to do my best to act when He calls me to act. Not out of fear and not out of striving, but just because the life He has planned is the best life that I can possibly live. I want to do it to bring Him glory and expand His kingdom here on earth. The life He has planned for me is designed for me to impact specific people and increase His kingdom in a specific way. Writing this book will have a ripple effect. One person may read it and be inspired to answer their call and change the world! That impact alone would be worth it. On this side of heaven, I won't know the full impact that it will have but I believe it will be revealed on the other side and what a glorious day that will be!

Something happens as He speaks; his words create. Genesis 1:3 NLT says *"Then God said 'Let there be light." and there was light."* He created with His words. This same thing is happening in you when He speaks to you about your future. His words have a creative impact on your life. Suddenly your future looks different. New possibilities suddenly open up. God doesn't speak without purpose, to fill the silence like we do at times. He speaks to create, to fill, to change our destinies, to bring His Kingdom to earth.

Consider for a moment, the power in his words. In Luke 5:27 *Jesus says to Levi the tax collector "Follow me"*. What happens next? In vs 28 *Levi got up and left everything and followed him*.

Levi had a lot to lose by leaving everything. The tax collectors were wealthy, they enjoyed a good lifestyle at the expense of the people. The words of Jesus changed lives, they changed people when they responded to them. **His words had the power to radically transform the identity and direction of the people he spoke to. His words have power.** I encourage you to respond when He speaks and allow him to change you and your future.

Yet most of us react with disbelief and doubt. We react more like Gideon than Levi. Like Gideon in Judges 6:15, we see ourselves as small and weak. We tell ourselves that we are being silly and shouldn't think so big. We try to forget what God is saying so we don't have to act or change course. His words fall to the ground lifeless and void. What happens when we choose to believe him and allow the words to create a new future? New life is breathed into us and a new future is formed. **Allow yourself to believe that it is possible, agree with what is being spoken and allow it to take shape.** He will begin to reveal His path and the way to you. It's quite likely that you won't know right away what it is going to look like or how you will do it but He will show you if you start asking and listening.

"You make known to me the path of life; you fill me with joy in your presence, with eternal pleasures at your right hand."
Psalm 16:11 NIV

Trust that the path to His best life for you will be made known. Stand on that word. On His path you will find joy in His presence. When you are walking with Him, you will feel His presence with you. His presence brings full joy. It's incredible to me that we resist His path so much. We serve a good God; His path isn't easy but it is good and it is what's best for us. Fill us Lord with your joy in your presence. As we choose to walk the path you have planned for us, fill us with joy!

Do we really need Him if we aren't taking any action in our life? One way to get really close to God is to start acting on what He wants you to do in your life. If we are always playing it safe and comfortable, we don't really need Him. We don't need to seek His direction in our life or even hear His voice. If we really need Him, we will seek Him and His direction. As a result, we will get really close to God, seeking his will and relying on His strength. If you want to get closer, start moving and taking some risks. You will need Him more than you ever have. You will need to walk hand in hand with Him to get there. You will need to allow Him to mould you and change you. The person you are today isn't the person you need to be to get there. You are going to need to change and you are going to have to connect with Him more often for that change to happen.

We all have things that hold us back – fears, doubts, hurts, and beliefs – that keep us from living our most abundant life. That will never change. We will always have something trying to hold us back. A nagging little voice that wants to convince us to stay small, hold back, play it safe. That's why we need to connect with God's voice to overcome it. **If we get so close to Him that we hear His voice and what He is saying about our lives and our future, then we can overcome the doubt.** Choosing to live a courageous life that is yielded to His will, will bring you closer to Him than you can ever imagine.

If you are not connected to a group of believers trained in the prophetic, find a group to get connected to. You need to be around people who seek His presence, hear from Him, and have the courage to speak it. This will equip you and encourage you in your journey with Him.

If you aren't sure where to go to find these types of believers, then start to pray for it. Ask God to help you find them. They are out there, and more and more churches are embracing the power of the Holy Spirit and equipping people in this area. Even more importantly, seek Him, seek Him with all your heart. The word promises in Jeremiah 29:13 *You will seek me and find me when you seek me with all your heart.* Get into His word and spend time in prayer. Seek the plans that He has for your life and you will find them. Trust that the Lord will reveal them to you.

– chapter 14 –

THERE WILL ALWAYS BE REASONS NOT TO

YOU MIGHT CALL them reasons; I might call them excuses. They are always there, the excuses, telling you why you can't do it now. Many of them are legitimate and logical. If you had to defend your decision not to act now, you could easily convince someone that you have a legitimate reason. You could find many to agree with your decision to wait. At least that's what you tell yourself. "I will wait until later, when the timing is better." Rarely does the timing get better. There is always something happening in our lives that we can use as an excuse. I have never met someone that has said "It's a perfect time to add something big to my life, I just have so much time." I am sure there is one or two out there somewhere, I just haven't met them yet.

You cannot let your excuses get in the way. If God is telling you to do it, then there is a way. If God is asking you to start, then you must begin. He will instruct you along the way. There may be something you are doing now that He will ask you to give up, so you can take on what He really wants you to do. Sometimes we take on responsibilities that are good, but they aren't our responsibilities. If you are one of those people that everyone can rely on to do anything, this might resonate with you. **You**

aren't meant to do everything; you are meant to do something specific that God is calling you to. Taking on too many other things may be your way of avoiding what He really wants you to do. We can fill our lives with a lot of distractions that seem good at the time, but they are keeping you from the best that God has for you. You may have to give up the good to go for the great. We often settle for good when what we could have is great. This is a good time to evaluate that. What responsibilities have you taken on that you are not meant to take on? What could you give up, making more room for what God wants?

You might be telling yourself that there is no way you could give up whatever you have committed to doing. You would feel like you are letting people down. You might feel like there isn't anyone else to do it. So, I ask you a question, **would you rather let people down or God down?** He is asking you to do something and if He is asking then it is important. Why are we so quick to do things for others but put God on hold? Isn't His opinion of you way more important than the opinions of others? Isn't his assignment on your life more important than some of these responsibilities?

Now I am not suggesting that you let everyone down and drop everything in an instant, that wouldn't be wise. I am just asking you to evaluate everything that you have taken on, and simplify your life, so that you can do more of what God wants you to do. Make some room in your life for the call that is on it. In my business life, I coach people on how to build a successful business and so often I have this thought "They are so busy being broke that they don't have time to be successful." What are you 'too busy' doing? Is it aligned with what you really want and what God genuinely wants for your life? Is it just a distraction? Answering this question honestly opens the door to living another way. Living aligned with God's will.

This means you will have to rearrange your life a little bit. Start with one thing. Be honest with those involved. Tell them that you need to simplify your life so that you can pursue what God really wants you to do. Assure them that you are not trying to be irresponsible or leave them in a bad position, but you need to prioritize and make room for what God is calling you to do. Give them the opportunity to find someone else to take on your responsibilities. There are others out there that can help and are willing. We convince ourselves that we are the only ones that can or will do all these things that we do. It feeds our ego and makes us feel important, but it doesn't change the fact that we may or may not be doing what God wants us to focus on. If you are honest with people and explain why, chances are they will be able to find someone else to take on what needs to be done. And who knows, maybe it will give that person a purpose, and that feeling of accomplishment, that they have been waiting for. Possibly by taking on something that wasn't yours to take on, you stood in the way of someone else finding what they were meant to do.

It is critical that you make God's will for your life a priority. You cannot put Him last on the list and truly live the abundant life that He has planned for you. What He has for you is better than anything you can plan, or anyone else can plan. Trust Him with your life. Some people won't understand. They won't see it the way that you see it. Their beliefs are like lenses through which they see the world and judge your decisions. You will not make everyone happy. You can't. **In fact, if you are making everyone else happy, you likely aren't following God, you are likely following people.** Often in our quest to make others happy, we don't end up making ourselves happy. It's okay if some people don't understand, God understands, and He is walking through this with you. He will give you supporters and cheerleaders to help you along the way. Likeminded people that see what you are trying to accomplish and encourage you.

You have some hard work to do now, reflect on what you have taken on that you need to put down so you can pursue the abundant life that God has for you. Pick up your journal and reflect on all that you are doing and pray about what God really wants you to do. What could you put down to live for Him? Seek Him above all else and He will help you identify what needs to go.

Move through the Resistance.

As you make changes and move towards your best life, you will encounter resistance within yourself. You will bump up against your limiting beliefs and fears and you will want to stop. I want to encourage you to push through the resistance. This is so important. Many people are too afraid to start but of those who start, many of them stop as soon as they feel that resistance. You need to push through when you feel that resistance. You can't let fear take over. You did not come this far to only come this far. Remember, resistance makes you stronger. In fitness training, we use weights to increase the resistance to build stronger bodies. Moving through the resistance to change will also make you stronger.

Often when people feel this resistance, they start looking for excuses to stop. They come up with all sorts of reasons. **The resistance is not a sign that you should quit, it is truly a sign that you must keep going.** I have learned to recognize it in myself and now have a desire to push through it. I know that if I push through something great will happen. This is a time where you need to pray and seek God more than ever. It is also a time to move and make things happen. You might be shaking and afraid, but the Lord is with you and will help you through it. You feel this way because it is human nature to avoid change. This resistance is a gift. Use the resistance as a tool to identify your fears and limitations. When you can identify what limits you, you can overcome it. When you start to recognize your fears, they have less power over you. It is an opportunity to breakthrough what holds you back.

What happens to our dreams and callings is a lot like what happens in the Parable of the Sower in Matthew 13. The farmer sows his seeds just like God places in us the great and wonderful things he is calling us to. Some of the seeds fall on the path and right away the birds snatch them up. We dismiss the ideas or dreams that come to us so quickly because it seems impossible or unrealistic and they have no time to take root and grow.

Some of the seeds fall in the shallow soil by rocks and start to grow but are scorched by the hot sun because they have no roots. This is like the dreams that we recognize and hold onto for a little while. We daydream about them a little while but never take any action towards them. Our doubts and indecision are like the rocks that prevent them from taking root.

Sometimes the seed falls in the thorns and is choked out. The seed begins to grow but the thorns choke it out. This is like the dream that we start to pursue but each step of the way fear chokes it out until we eventually just give up. Some of those thorns come from inside of us, our fears and insecurities. Some of the thorns come from well-meaning friends or family that want to protect us and unknowingly choke out our dreams with discouragement.

Some seed falls in the good soil and produces a crop of thirty, sixty or one hundred- fold. These are the dreams that are pursued and acted upon with perseverance and faith. They are watered, fertilized and the weeds are pulled. These are the plants that are protected and nurtured. Protect your dream from the weeds of doubt and fear that threaten to choke them out. Faith is the fertilizer, believing it is possible, believing that God will help you. As you decide to pursue what God is calling you to do, there will always be birds, rocks, weeds, and thorns that threaten to steal your dream and get in the way. Keep watering, fertilizing, and pulling the weeds and watch the harvest of abundance grow!

– *chapter 15* –

NOW GO AHEAD, LIVE LIFE ABUNDANTLY

Now all has been heard; here is the <u>conclusion</u> of the matter: Fear God and keep his commandments, for this is the duty of all mankind. Ecclesiastes 12:13

I HAVE SHARED with you my journey and some of the lessons learned in my pursuit of God's abundance in my life and here is the conclusion. I hope you have been inspired and equipped to LIVE LIFE ABUNDANTLY! You only have one life to live and how you choose to live it matters. You have the choice now to step into all that you were created to be or hold back and play small. As Marianne Williamson wrote "Your playing small does not serve the world." **God has given you the precious gift of life and your gift back to him is to live it well.** To live it seeking all that he has planned for you. Live it in abundance. Our God is an abundant God.

Life is short. We do not know how many years God will give us on this earth. For some we may have decades and for others just a few more years. Ask yourself questions like these,

1. If I only had a few more years to have an impact on this world, what impact would I want to have?
2. What would I regret not doing if my time were to come earlier than expected?
3. What talents and gifts did God give me to use to impact the world and how can I start using them?

The keys to your most abundant life live in the answers to these questions. My hope for you is that you will ponder these questions and allow yourself to believe that you can live that life. If you aren't sure what the answers are to these questions, start asking God. Seek and you will find. Ask and you shall receive.

I believe that as you begin to live your best life, you will draw closer to God. **You will need to rely on Him more and more as you take risks and discover who you were created to be.** You will need to seek Him and hear His voice. You will experience his faithfulness, blessing, and presence in a new fresh way. As you get closer to Him, you will begin to see who you really are in Him. Your identity in Him. Walking with God in pursuit of your dreams is an adventure. You never know where He might take you. I am excited for you and what lies ahead!

There will be obstacles and challenges along the way. It won't always be easy. Rejoice in those obstacles for they refine you and strengthen you.

> *Consider it pure joy, my brothers and sisters, whenever you face trials of many kinds, because you know that the testing of your faith produces perseverance. Let perseverance finish its work so that you may be mature and complete, not lacking anything. James 1:2 – 4*

God uses these challenges to prepare you for what is ahead. The difficulties do not mean that you won't get there or that you are on the wrong path. It is only when we are tested and challenged that we grow. So, consider it pure joy that the God of heaven loves you enough to prepare you for what is ahead. He will not let you move ahead unprepared. Thank you, Jesus! Praise him through the obstacles and trials. Ask him to teach you and change you as you walk through each challenge.

Let's get started with just one step. **What is one thing you can start doing right away to move closer to the life God is calling you to?** Once you identify just one thing, go for it! Do it now! Procrastination has killed more dreams than anything else. I have learned that when God gives you an idea, you need to act on it right away. The longer we wait, the more likely it is that we will talk ourselves out of it. Waiting to start is not going to help you refine the idea or make it better. Doing it will help you figure it out. We tell ourselves that we need to wait and develop this detailed plan before we start but starting will help us develop the idea. We can get lost in the planning and never DO anything. So go ahead take that first step!

My dream for you, my friends, is that when your time has come and you go to be with Jesus, that you will leave a legacy of dreams lived and fulfilled. That you will have emptied out all the potential inside you in a life well lived! That when they bury you, that your grave will be empty because you have lived the dreams and potential inside you. I pray that they will not be buried with your physical body in the ground. I am praying that the richest place on earth will no longer be the graveyard!

Lastly, I leave you with this poem. God gave me this vision of what it looks like to God when we reject our dreams.

The Rejected Dream

Rejected and alone the Dream shrinks back
It falls away and gets quiet
Like the rejected child whose voice is not heard.
Then God whispers,
"Try again, don't give up."
Courageously, the Dream pushes away the hurt and tries again.
Trying to remind you of why you were born
Whispering in your ear
Of the difference you are supposed to make.
For just a moment, you listen,
You are filled with joy and hope.
One small victory
Once again, the Dream is filled
With hope of a future fulfilled.

Until Doubt and Fear awaken once more
They push the Dream out of your mind.
The Dream watches as Doubt and Fear push you around
Tears fall as the Dream listens
They're lying and discouraging
Stealing your confidence.
Stealing your future like thieves in the night.
Holding you down with their chains of lies and deceit.
"You aren't good enough" you hear them say.
"Not strong enough,
Not smart enough,
Not rich enough to live your Dream.
You are not enough."
You listen to their lies
This makes them stronger.

It feeds them like a hungry beast.
Slowly you shrink and they get bigger.
You believe their lies
They speak louder.
They make their home
In your mind and thoughts
A permanent dwelling
So hard to tear down.

The Dream tries to come back
Each time it is pushed out by Doubt and Fear
Until it tires and falls to the ground
Rejected, forgotten and alone

Unless you learn to turn Doubt and Fear away
Like intruders at the gate.
Unless you close it
Lock it behind them.
Unless you give the Dream a louder, stronger voice
To drown them out.
Unless you take the Dream by the hand and dance some more
Listening for its quiet whispers of hope
Unless you quietly say "What if…"
Unless you breathe more life into your dream.
Unless you take those first small steps.

Slowly Doubt and Fear will fade away
A shadow of what they once were.
Weaker, quieter.
They look for a chance and try again
But they know it's all in vain
For the Dream is favored, protected, cherished.
They see you dancing eye to eye in perfect rhythm

Like lovers alone on a crowded dance floor
They can't steal your attention any longer
They can't cut in and take over.
Your eyes are locked on your Dream in perfect unison.
Soon your dance is one of joy.
You are truly living
That's all you've ever wanted.
To be alive; strong and happy.
Fully embracing the gifts God gave you.
Living LIFE ABUNDANTLY.
© Arlene Zandbelt

Call to Action

If you are reading this and do not know Jesus or have a personal relationship with him, I hope this book has introduced him to you. I hope it has caused you to wonder about a God that cares enough to pursue you and set you free from whatever is holding you back. Not a God that judges and controls. Not a God that limits you. I want you to know that God loves you more than your human brain can imagine. His love is beyond the limits of our imagination. He understands who you are and what makes you unique better than anyone, even you. He knows exactly why you were born and what unique abilities and talents that live in you. **You may not know God, but *He knows you*. You may not believe in Him, but *He believes in you*!** He knows exactly why you were born and what great plans he has for you.

If you don't know God and want to know Him and the abundant life he has planned for you, you can just say this prayer and start your walk with Him.

Jesus, I want to know you. I want to know the deep, unending love you have for me. I ask you to come into my life. I have made mistakes in the past so please forgive me and help me walk in a new way with you. Amen

If you have said the prayer above, welcome to the family of God, and welcome to a new and abundant life. Please connect with me on the following platforms, I would love to help you become connected and start your journey with God.

Facebook: @arlenezandbelt
Instagram @Arlenelivesabundantly

My friends, I leave you with one last word of encouragement from Joshua 1:9 NIV

Have I not commanded you? Be strong and courageous. Do not be afraid; do not be discouraged, for the Lord your God will be with you wherever you go.

God is with you wherever you go. Stand strong in him and you truly can live life abundantly. Embrace the beautiful adventure that lies ahead of you! May the Lord bless each step that you take and fill you with strength and courage along the way. I pray that you have dreams and visions that inspire your imagination. I pray you feel his presence and his peace as you take each step.
Now go live life and live it abundantly.

INNER HEALING RESOURCES

Elijah House- an inner healing ministry that helps people get to the root of their pain through the power of the Holy Spirit. Hand in hand with the Holy Spirit and the Lord's guidance, they are seeing people set free.

https://elijahhouse.org/pages/prayer-ministry
Or call 1-208-900-9160

Heartsync Ministries- based on the idea that there are four main parts of our hearts and that all of us have parts that are affected by trauma. When Jesus interacts with the parts that are holding the pain and trauma, it releases a new freedom for the person.

https://heartsyncministries.org/ministry/

ARLENE ZANDBELT grew up in rural Alberta in a somewhat conservative family, where the women took on more traditional roles. As the youngest daughter of an entrepreneur, Arlene always knew she wanted more. This desire drove her to finish college, move to the city and build a successful business in finance.

She now lives in the foothills near Calgary, AB where her husband, 2 sons, 2 horses, and 2 Bernese Mountain dogs enjoy their life surrounded by nature. Arlene's strong faith in God has allowed her to believe that anything is possible and has given her the strength to pursue the abundant life God has for her. She has a strong desire to inspire and empower others to live life to the fullest seeking the best that God has planned for them.

ARLANA ZANDT began her life in rural Alberta in a conservative family where the woman took on more traditional roles. As the youngest daughter of an entrepreneur, Arlana always knew she had a choice. This choice drove her to finish college, move to the city and build a successful business in finance. She now lives in the foothills near Calgary, AB with her husband, son, a horse and 3 retired Mountain dogs enjoying their life surrounded by nature. A friend among faith in God has allowed her to believe that anything is possible and has given her the strength to pursue the abundant life God has for her. She has a strong desire to inspire and empower others to live life to the fullest, seeking the best that God has planned for them.